VICTORINOX
SWISS ARMY

D1495148

SWISS ARMY KNIFE

WHITTLING
IN THE WILD

30+ Fun & Useful Things to Make Out of Wood

Felix Immler

Photography by Matthew Worden

FOX CHAPEL
PUBLISHING

This book was created in collaboration with Victorinox AG, Ibach-Schwyz, Switzerland.

NOTE: Be aware of all the laws concerning outdoor activities where you live, including laws about slingshots, bows, arrows, catapults, and boomerangs as well as plant and animal conservation laws. Children should always be supervised by adults if allowed to use or make slingshots and other shooting or throwing objects. When throwing or slinging an object, always know your target and what's behind it. Do not shoot at hard surfaces or at the surface of water. Objects may bounce off or ricochet and hit someone or something you had not intended to hit.

Visit Felix Immler's website and YouTube channel:
🏠 *www.feliximmler.ch*
▶ YouTube *www.youtube/feliximmler*

Schnitz it Yourself
by Felix Immler
ISBN 978-3-03800-980-1
Copyright © 2019 by AT Verlag, Aarau and Munich, Switzerland
English language edition © 2020 by Fox Chapel Publishing Company, Inc., 903 Square Street, Mount Joy, PA 17552.

Photography by Matthew Worden

ISBN 978-1-4971-0071-8

Library of Congress Control Number: 2020931483

To learn more about the other great books from Fox Chapel Publishing, or to find a retailer near you, call toll-free 800-457-9112 or visit us at *www.FoxChapelPublishing.com*.

We are always looking for talented authors. To submit an idea, please send a brief inquiry to acquisitions@foxchapelpublishing.com.

Printed in Singapore
First printing

Contents

Basics and Techniques

Foreword

Many people are happy with using their Victorinox Swiss Army Knife to simply shave the bark off a branch or whittle a sharp point on a stick. Those who are a bit more ambitious want some great project ideas. Most people are only aware of about four whittling projects: the walking stick, the roasting spit, the slingshot, and the archery bow. They may not consider any other possibilities. In this book, I would like to show you thirty-three unique project ideas to open the door to infinite possibilities and give you the inspiration to match your ambition. Compared to my first book, *Crafting with the Pocket Knife*, this book focuses less on classic projects like forks, spoons, and a spinning top. It also isn't about whittling tools for camping like my second book, *Outdoors with a Swiss Army Knife*. This book contains unique projects that are slightly more demanding. They are a collection of my personal favorite projects, toys, instruments, and everyday items. Who ever thought of making a balloon saxophone or a crossbow with a Swiss Army Knife? How do you build an apple slingshot, a parachute, or a catapult?

It has brought me much joy to develop these projects. Collecting ideas, tinkering, and developing projects are my absolute favorite parts of my profession as a Swiss Army Knife expert. I created each project at least ten times myself before I could be sure it was ready for this book. I spent months working on the best approaches and techniques. I whittled an equivalent of two trees' worth of wood and sticks before I got the projects to be the way I wanted them for this book. I created what seemed like a ton of practice projects, and some of the "guinea pigs" were ultimately rejected.

My three children and I appreciate the objects and toys we've made ourselves much more than those manufactured for store shelves. Each unique piece contains a unique part of nature, passionately designed and built by hand. It is a true representation of my craft, in the very literal sense.

So, let's get started! Everything you need to create your one-of-a-kind projects can be found in nature, in your home, or even in the trash. The only tool you need is the Victorinox Swiss Army Knife with a saw attachment.

I wish you luck and lots of success!

—*Felix Immler*

"Happiness is not something ready made. It comes from your own actions."

—*Dalai Lama*

Introduction

Why Another Whittling Book?

All my projects are unique, and they can all be made using the Victorinox Swiss Army Knife with a saw attachment. Every other whittling book I know calls for other tools like handsaws, drills, files, gouges, hammers, or axes—but not this book. I love whittling with the Swiss Army Knife because it allows me to be spontaneous and work almost anywhere at any time.

This book contains new whittling project ideas you won't find in any other book. For months I developed many new projects as well as updated existing projects to require only a Swiss Army Knife. The ideas came from friends, workshop participants, YouTubers, or myself. A few classics such as the slingshot, the willow flute, and the raft can be found here as well. Because I often see my own ideas being copied, I think it is very important to give credit to the people whose ideas influenced these projects.

With over 700 photos and illustrations (and the videos on my YouTube channel), I explain the projects and techniques in this book with detailed step-by-step instructions. To make sure the pictures in this book make the instructions as easy to understand as possible, I joined forces with professional photographer Matthew Worden. He accompanied me through forests and fields for weeks while I developed my favorite projects. Thank you so much, Matthew! You are great!

Child's Play?

Around 20 (!) new whittling books have been published in German since my first carving book, *Working with a Swiss Army Knife*, went on the market in 2012. Whittling appears to be experiencing a big increase in popularity. Most of these books are made for children or beginners. They often contain the same

projects and attempt to show how easy it is to get started. This book has a completely different message: whittling is not that easy! This is especially the case if you want to take on a project any more difficult than the roasting spit.

Whittling is a wonderful hobby for young and old. Even today, whittling with a Swiss Army Knife still captivates many children. Completely analog and battery-free, it is a companion for adventures big and small and creates valuable experiences outside of the digital world. It is creative and practical, and invites you to engage with nature. I personally have found so much joy in it that I have made it my profession. Whittling requires endurance, strength, fine-motor skills, knowledge of natural materials, imagination, and much more. Children who want to get involved need focus, concentration, the right knife, and suitable projects. They have to practice often and be able to rely on a good, patient teacher. My experience from well over three hundred workshops has shown me that it is important to work closely with children when whittling. In order for them to really develop creative ideas, they need more than just being given a stick and a Swiss Army Knife. Many children want to start working on "cool" projects right away, like the apple slingshot or the paddle steamer. This only works, however, with the active help of a skilled adult whittler who can show the child how it's done if he or she is struggling. With a good role model and a satisfying goal in reach, children become more inclined to keep at it and practice the necessary techniques. Whittling as a team is fun and helps strengthen your relationship.

For Kids and Adults Working Together
Novice whittlers who have never held a Swiss Army Knife before will become quickly overwhelmed by the projects in this book. Even children who already have some experience will quickly reach their limits. This does not mean, however, that this book is unsuitable for children. On the contrary, the idea behind this

book is that children should always work with an adult, which has a great positive side effect. Nothing helps create a stronger bond than working together to achieve a common goal—a wonderful opportunity to build relationships between two generations.

In this regard, the book is meant for whittling enthusiasts of all ages. The selected projects appeal to children just as much as adults, but the techniques require fine-motor skills and often also technical understanding.

Sizes and Dimensions

In general, all of the projects in this book can be made larger or smaller than specified. In nature you have to work with the material that you can find. For this reason, my instructions focus on the procedure, the functional principle, and relative dimensions of each project. My instructions are not meant to be read as recipe-like steps with strict size requirements.

This book should also be a source of inspiration to help you practice techniques. It describes tricks and tips and should hopefully inspire you to practice, to develop your own unique style, and to create your own designs. All projects have multiple ways of reaching the same goal. Be brave! Be creative! The instructions in this book describe just some of many possibilities.

Videos and Instructions

So that you don't have to take the entire book with you into the forest, you can download videos and instructions from my YouTube channel and website to your mobile phone. You can start your carving adventure in the forest with just a Swiss Army Knife and smartphone in your pocket! The videos that show, for example, how the whistle sounds or how far the flinging arrow flies can also be found in the playlist "Schnitz it yourself" on my YouTube channel.

▶ YouTube www.youtube.com/feliximmler
🏠 www.feliximmler.ch

The Right Knife

I used the Victorinox Huntsman Swiss Army Knife for all projects in this book. In general, any Victorinox model with a saw, awl, small blade, and large blade would be suitable. A Swiss Army Knife with scissors is very practical for many projects but isn't absolutely necessary. Because I have to draw or make markings for most of my projects, I replaced one side of my Swiss Army Knife with a handle that contains a pen and penholder. If you want to add one to your Swiss Army Knife as well, you can find it in the accessories section of any Victorinox retail store or on the Victorinox website (*www.victorinox.com*).

Almost all handles have a slot for a pin next to the corkscrew (see picture 20 on page 84). Because a pin can be helpful for some projects, I added a Victorinox pin as well. The knife can also be fitted with an ordinary needle from your household sewing kit.

Of course, larger Victorinox Swiss Army Knives from the 111mm series or the 130mm series can be also used for the projects in this book. I personally do not prefer the larger Swiss Army Knives because they don't have a small knife for very fine work, which is really important to me.

The Go-To Tools in My Backpack

Along with the Swiss Army Knife, I always carry string and a lighter. Many projects require the use of string. I prefer to use natural string like hemp, jute, or flax. This way I don't have to feel guilty if I, for example, leave a waterwheel in a stream because I know the string will decompose naturally if the wheel is washed away. Ever since my wife showed me her trick using a hot glue stick and a lighter, I've always carried them with me as well. If you use a lighter to heat the end of a hot glue stick until it is transparent and softened, it becomes a great way to seal cracks or glue things together. And hot glue hardens again very quickly, which is really practical.

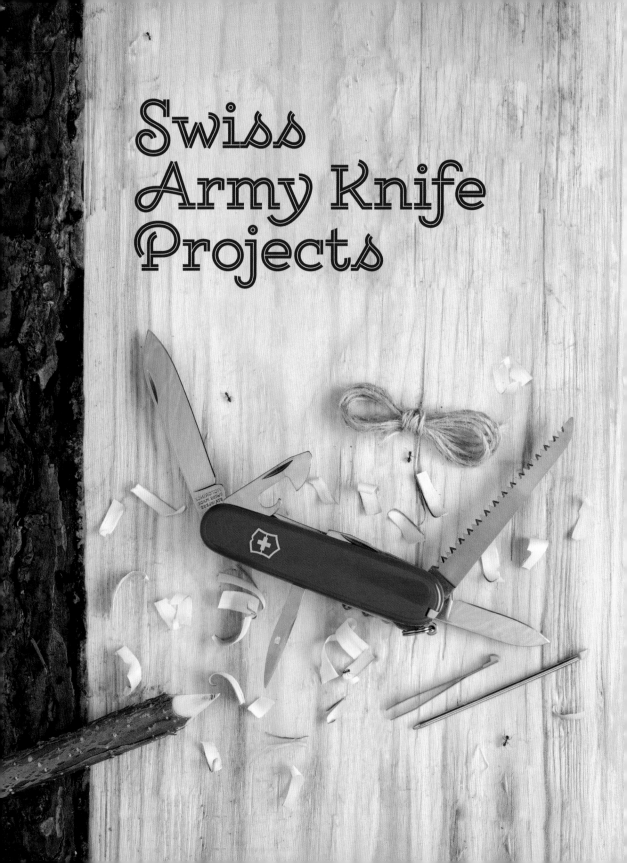

Swiss Army Knife Projects

Things That Float, Splash, Write, and Spin

POP-POP BOAT

As a child, I was always fascinated by steam engines. My father had a metal workshop. When I was about ten years old, we built a steam engine together. That's when I learned how a steam engine really works. Years later, I bought a pop-pop boat during a trip to India. I was absolutely fascinated by its simplicity and how it worked. The motor does not need any moving parts such as pistons, valves, or wheels. Its energy source is merely a candle. The idea is simple: water in a tube closed on one side is heated by the candle. The water evaporates, requiring more space, and forces the evaporated water to be expelled through the opening. A vacuum is therefore created in the tube. This draws more water into the tube to be heated. Because the water is expelled in once direction, but is drawn in from all directions by the negative pressure, forward momentum is created.

As I was considering projects for this book, I remembered the pop-pop boat. I thought, "There must be a way to simplify this candle motor so that it can be created with a Swiss Army Knife," so I got to work. After a few attempts, I made it work.

What You Need

To implement this project, you need an aluminum can to make the pipe, a piece of bark or soft wood for the boat hull, a tea light or a candle stub, a lighter, and a Swiss Army Knife.

1. Cut open an empty aluminum can with the knife blade or scissors, and bend it back by pulling the metal against the direction of the can's curve, so that you now have a more or less flat aluminum rectangle in front of you.

2. Fold the aluminum sheet in half, and flatten the fold with two pieces of wood.

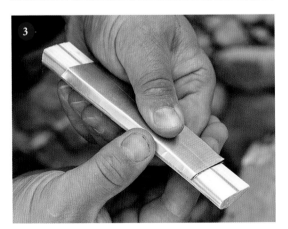

3. Draw an isosceles trapezoid so that the longer bottom 2" (5cm) side is aligned with the folded edge and the shorter 1¼" (3cm) side is at the open edge. I carefully carved the contour into the sheet. Drawing with a waterproof pen would be even better. Then, use scissors to cut out the trapezoid and bend out a strip about ³⁄₁₆" (5mm) wide on both sides. To ensure that the bended edge is as straight as possible, bend the metal around the edge of a block of wood.

4. The corners on the longer base side are particularly at risk: they tend to open up and get loose. To prevent this, heat up the aluminum with a lighter before you fold it completely.

5. On the other side, bend a ³⁄₁₆" (5mm) wide strip 180°. Now bend both sides 90°.

6. Again, it is recommended to heat the corner of the folded base side. Now open the gap on the short base side with a stick. Place the stick into the opening to form a tube.

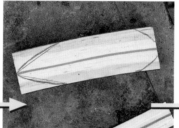

7. Now you need an approximately 6" (15.2cm) long boat hull. To make whittling easier and make the boat more buoyant, I recommend using poplar bark or softwood. To ensure that the boat drives straight, the hull needs to be as symmetrical as possible.

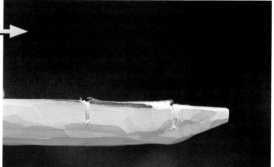

8. Trace the diameter of the tea light or the candle at the back of the boat and saw two ⁵⁄₁₆" (8mm) deep grooves on either side.

9. You can remove the wood pretty easily by placing a screwdriver in the center of the groove and prying it out with a bit of force. After you've done that, you may need to whittle a bit of the area out so that the candle fits.

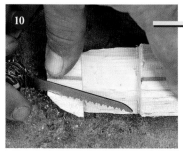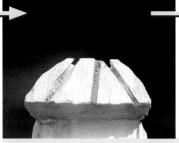

10. If you prefer not to pry, you can simply whittle the whole area out entirely and simply lift it from the hull. Saw two grooves into the rear to create a dovetail where you can insert the tube you created.

Tip

These cuts are a bit tricky because you have to hold the saw blade diagonally in two directions. First, saw both cuts a bit too close together so that the tube doesn't yet fit. Then, carefully expand the width of the cuts a very small amount each time until the tube can be inserted into the opening.

11. The boat is now complete!

12. The tube must be filled with water before you can place a burning candle underneath it. A syringe filled with water makes this a bit easier. With the remaining aluminum sheet, you could build a windbreak since your boat will be very susceptible to wind. Once it gets windy, the candle motor doesn't work quite as planned. The pop-pop boat always drives well indoors (for example, in a bathtub) or in a sheltered pond. Ship ahoy!

PROJECT

REED BOAT

As a child, I loved playing with toy boats in the bathtub. This fascination seems to be hereditary because my boys love it as well. They play with a little ship or a motorized police boat. But what I enjoy most is when they play with a boat they built themselves and get lost in the fun of it.

In my opinion, the hardest part of building a boat is making the hull. First, finding the right material is often difficult, and second, making the hull the right shape when all you have is a Swiss Army Knife is a lot of work. It is easier, however, to make a hull out of reed. The following instructions will explain exactly how it's done.

What You Need

1. The hull is made up of three bundles of reeds knotted together. For a bundle, I collect enough reeds so that they're the size of my thumb and forefinger wrapped around them. Now tie each individual bundle together by wrapping the string tightly around it three times. One wrap around is in the middle and the other two are 4" (10cm) to the left and to the right of the middle.

To make a reed boat, you'll first need a bundle of reeds for the hull, a straight branch for a mast and boom (a pole that stabilizes the bottom of the sail), some string, a stone for the keel, a sail, and a Swiss Army Knife. The size of the boat and the length of the hull are up to you. In this example, I will build a boat that is about 20" (.5m) long.

2. Now saw off any protruding reeds so that the hull is about 20" (50cm) long.

3. Because the front and back of a boat are thinner than the middle, cut each bundle a little bit thinner toward the ends to create a taper.

6. Now attach another piece of string, as tight as possible, around the front and back of the boat.

7. This piece of string should cover all three bundles. Now you've formed the final shape of the boat's hull. Because the last two pieces of string are wrapped around the tapered part of the boat, they tend to slip outward. To prevent this, you can tie both outer pieces together with a third piece of string lengthwise.

4. The middle 8" (20cm) of the hull should not be tapered.

5. After you have tied the first two bundles together with three wraps of the string, attach the third bundle. Wrap the string similarly around the same spots as with the first bundle. I recommend wrapping the string around the bundles several times. Take a pointed piece of wood to make enough space to pull the string through the first two bundles.

8. For the mast, use a sturdy branch that's slightly longer than the boat's hull. Place the mast through the middle bundle where you prefer.

9. It should extend about 6" (15cm) underneath the boat.

10. Carefully split the branch (facing the front of the boat).

11. Clamp a flat stone between it. Secure the stone at the top and bottom with a piece of string.

12. Now it's the sail's turn. I use a doggy waste bag as a sail. You can, of course, use other materials, like cloth. In any case, the sail's material needs to be as light as possible. To make a sail out of a bag, gather the upper open corners of the bag and tie them together with a knot.

13. Now the bag already has the shape of a sail. Next, attach the sail to the mast at your desired height. Push the pointed ends of the boom through the bottom corners of the bag.

14. The sail should be slightly arched. Then tie the lower corners of the sail firmly to the boom.

17. Now you can set your reed boat in the water. If the boat does not go straight, you can attach a whittled rudder to the bottom of the back of the boat. If you would like to build a really big reed boat that is big enough for you to sit in and paddle around, you'll find a great video about exactly that on my YouTube channel called "Building Instructions for a Reed Boat."

15. Connect the knots with a piece of string to the back of the boat. This line should be loose enough that the boom can turn a little around the mast and catch the wind.

16. Secure the boom loosely to the mast so that the boom can rotate.

RAFT

In my first book, *Crafting with the Pocket Knife*, there are instructions for building a raft. For this, I tied the lengthwise branches to the raft platform with string. If these were not tied very tightly or if the wood shrank when it dried, the platform would unfortunately quickly become unstable and shaky, causing the raft to fall apart when using it.

I would like to show you a much more stable version of this raft—one with a dovetail joint. In my opinion, the dovetail method is even easier than tying all the sticks together. Also, it's a great chance to practice your sewing technique with your Swiss Army Knife.

What You Need

To build this raft, you need seven straight branches for the lengthwise section of the raft. They should be as dry as possible. One slightly thinner branch and one slightly thicker one will be needed for the crossbeams. For the mast and boom, you need two rods (hazel wood works well), a few feet (about a meter) of string, and a sail. Of course, you'll also need your Swiss Army Knife for this project.

1. The overall size of the raft is up to you. I cut the branches for the lengthwise section approximately 12" (30cm) long. Saw a dovetail groove in all seven lengthwise branches about 1½" (4cm) from the end.

2. To make the dovetail groove, begin sawing straight.

3. Then turn the blade slightly to cut inward from both directions as you go.

4. This forms a small, triangular hole that the thin cross branches can fit into.

5. If you continue to cut similar dovetail grooves into the remaining branches at the same point and line them up with the cross branches, you'll have a stable, slip-resistant platform for your raft. The side with the dovetail connection is the front (bow) of your raft.

6. Using the awl, make a hole through the middle branch to secure the mast. To make this easier, remove the six side branches before you begin. Leave the cross branch connected to help make sure the hole is at a proper right angle for the mast compared to the platform. Make the hole slightly off-center and closer to the front (the bow).

7. Now you can place the remaining lengthwise branches on the cross branch.

8. Saw the rear cross branch so that it sticks out approximately 1¼" (3cm) on both sides. Secure the rear cross branch to the top of the raft platform. Because the cross branch is on top and shouldn't dip into the water when the raft is floating, this will result in much less resistance.

9. Secure the lengthwise branches to the cross branch as shown. You can use any technique you like to do this as long as the platform is stable.

10. Also secure the lengthwise branches in the front (the bow) with string to prevent them from sliding.

11. Cut the thin cross branch so that it is slightly longer than the raft.

12. Next, make the mast. The length of the mast depends on the size of its sail.

13. Slightly taper the bottom of the mast so it best fits in the hole you made for it.

14. Now cut the sail to your desired size. For the sail, you can use cloth, plastic, or another material of your choosing. Small interwoven leaves as well as large leaves would be a very natural choice for a sail. If your sail is made of fabric, sew a hem through which you can later put the boom. To do this, fold the sail about 1¼" (3cm) along the narrow side, and sew the seam of the hem using the Swiss Army Knife sewing technique explained on page 198.

15. If you sewed a hem, you can now push the boom through it.

16. Then, split the mast at the top as shown in the photo.

17. Make sure not to do it like I did!

18. Then thread a piece of string through the gap. Wrap one end of the string around the left side of the mast, and insert it again into the gap. Wrap the other end of the string around of the right side of the mast and reinsert into the gap. Attach the string on the left and right to the crossbar. The knots will shift less if you whittle a circular groove at the end of each side.

19. Now tie a piece of string to each lower corner of the sail.

20. Tie the strings from the sail loosely to the rear cross branch.

21. Now your raft is ready to be christened for its maiden voyage. If you smash a bottle of champagne over the hull of this boat, however, I'm afraid you'll have to start over at step 1. Cheers!

WATER GUN

On hot summer days, there's nothing more refreshing than a fun water pistol fight. My friend Mauro Spadin, a creative whittler and outdoorsman, had the great idea of creating a water squirt gun out of an elder wood branch. Thanks, Mauro, for letting me take your idea and develop it into what eventually wound up in this book.

What You Need

To make this water gun, you need a straight piece of elder wood about 16" (40cm) long with a diameter of about ⅜" (1cm). For the piston, use a hazel sapling whose diameter is smaller than that of the elder wood piece. Additionally, you need some string and a Swiss Army Knife. If you have some resin and a lighter available, you can use it to seal your water gun's nozzle.

1. First, saw the elder wood to the desired length. In this example, I went with around 12" (30cm). There should be a natural bulge or branch-off point at the end of the piece. The diameter is somewhat smaller here. This prevents the water from shooting out of the wrong end of the tube when you use it.

2. Now remove some of the wood inside the stick to form the tube. You can remove the first 1½" (4cm) on each side with the corkscrew on your Swiss Army Knife.

3. The next 1¼" (3cm) of inside wood can be removed by turning the saw blade inside the branch. It's important to make sure you're pulling the wood out and not just compacting it inside the stick. Getting compressed wood out from the middle of the stick is very difficult, if not impossible, without more complicated tools.

4. Now, there's only about 6" (15cm) of wood you still need to remove. This would be easiest with a long drill, a thick wire, or a long wood screw. Since I've made it a point to not use such aids, I used a dried hardwood branch that I tapered with the Swiss Army Knife. I tried to remove the inside wood by carefully inserting the stick, spinning it, and pulling out the wood. This is bit tedious and requires both patience and careful movements. But it's absolutely doable. Removing inside wood from a freshly cut branch is easier than removing it from a dry branch. Once you've created a hole all the way through the branch, you can "scratch clean" the inner wall with the thinner branch. Once it's clean, the piston branch should be able to fit inside it with some maneuvering.

5. Cut a hole 1¼" (3cm) from the front end of the tube. First, cut a finger recess using the fine-cutting technique (see page 193). Then, make a hole with the awl. This hole serves as an air intake when water is being drawn in. When squirting the gun, cover the hole with your thumb.

6. Finally, wrap a piece of string around the front end of the branch 10 times and tie it off. This prevents the tube from breaking under pressure when in use.

7. Let's make the nozzle. Find a small hazel branch with a similar diameter and shape to the hole and cut it ½" (1.5cm) long. You may have to whittle the nozzle to fit properly. Now make a hole as small as possible in the nozzle so the water can shoot nice and far. Take the pin from your Swiss Army Knife and carefully insert it through the marrow of the to-be nozzle until it pokes through the other side. Now heat the pin with the lighter until it glows and slowly remove the pin through the back with tweezers. Repeat this process three times.

8. You're left with a clean hole that's smaller than 1/32" (1mm).

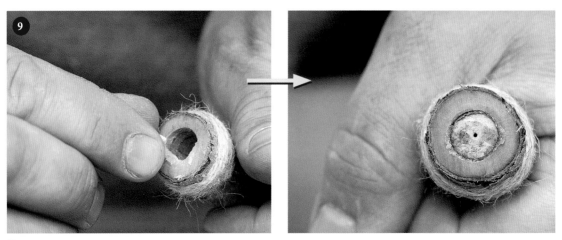

9. Brush a very little bit of resin on the inside of the tube before attaching the nozzle. Make sure you use enough force to press the nozzle into the tube. Otherwise, the water pressure may cause it to fly away.

10. Insert the nozzle 1/32" (1mm) into the tube, stick the pin into the nozzle hole to prevent it from getting clogged, and brush some more resin on the edges.

11. Melt the resin with the lighter.

12. Saw off a 4" (10cm) piece from the elder wood tube. This will become the handle for your piston. Now cut your piston rod to the proper length and remove the bark.

13. The piston rod extends from the beginning of the suction hole to the end of the handle. Form a slight point in the piston rod and press it into the handle until the rod is flush with the rear end of the handle. The piston rod and handle must be firmly attached.

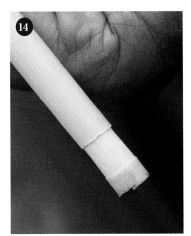

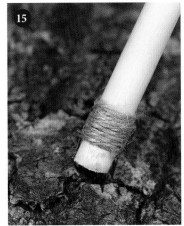

14. Cut a ⅜" (1cm)-wide groove around the piston rod about 2" (5mm) before the end. The groove only needs to be about ¼" (0.5mm) deep.

15. Now wrap string around to seal the connection. Start at the back of the groove and wrap the string around, laying each loop next to the previous one, as tight as possible, until it's the length of the groove. Then, do the same thing in reverse until you're back at the start. Now link the end to the beginning. Because the knot sticks out slightly, carefully whittle a small notch where the knot sits. Then, you can push the knot into it.

17. Give it a test. If the water comes out toward you instead of through the piston, remove the string and re-wrap it. Go back and forth twice this time. However, you can't completely prevent a little bit of water from hitting you as well as your target. If you want to tinker a bit more, you can try greasing the string with butter. It is quite possible that it will make your water gun a bit more leak-proof. But enough messing around. It's time to have fun in your next water gun fight!

16. Carefully insert the piston into the hole by twisting the two pieces against each other. Because of the taper at the beginning of the tube, this takes quite a bit of force. Once you've managed that, make sure the piston is tight enough. Keep in mind that the string will swell a bit when it gets wet.

EIGHT-BLADE WATERWHEEL

When I was a child, I really enjoyed spending time at the creek: building dams and bridges, fishing, swimming, throwing stones into the water or piling them up, making boats and rafts, as well as making waterwheels. And I still love all of these things today!

The eight-blade waterwheel has an impressive smoothness. Because there are always several blades in the water, this waterwheel has constant energy and enough power to move continuously. The size definitions are based on the waterwheel that I built for the photos in this book. I have, however, built functioning eight-blade waterwheels that were much smaller. As with many other projects, it's up to you how large or small you want to make it.

What You Need

For the blades of this waterwheel, you need two straight branches about 16" (40cm) long and with a diameter of about 1½" (4cm). For the axle, I used strong hazel saplings as straight as possible and two forked branches as a stand. One of the forks can also be reversed, like a hooked number 7. Naturally, the only tool I'm using for this project is a Swiss Army Knife.

1. Split both branches lengthwise to make the wheel blades. To find out more about how this works, you can read the section "Splitting wood with homemade wooden wedges" on page 191. I use birch wood for the wheel blades because they tend to have very little twisting as they grow.

2. After splitting, whittle the wood at the split as flat as possible. Split away some wood on the second rounded side of each piece by using the knife on the outer half. Otherwise, you risk the split going toward the middle instead of toward the outside.

3. Whittle the four boards to a final size of approximately ¼"–⁹⁄₃₂" (6–7mm) thick.

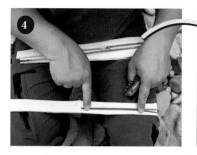

4. Now mark the center. If you don't have a measuring tool, you can use a blade of grass the same length as a board and fold it in the middle.

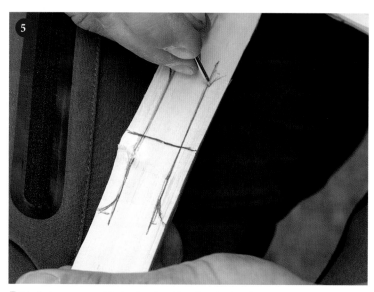

6. Whittle to create a tapered middle area.

5. Take the two narrower of the four boards and draw lines showing where to remove wood in the middle of the board. At the narrowest point, the board should be half as wide as at the ends.

7. Saw a groove in both boards up to the middle. You can simply break out the area between the cuts. The grooves in each board should be equally wide.

8. Both boards can now be inserted into each other to form a stable cross.

9. Mark the width of the grooves on the other two boards. The groove goes approximately to the very middle.

10. Saw along the markings and remove the wood. Since the groove will probably still be too small, whittle a 45° facet on both sides of the groove with the small blade.

11. Now you can bring the pieces together to form a star shape.

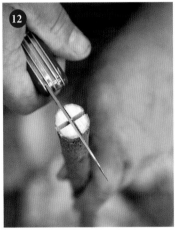

12. Begin to create a four-way split in the front, thicker side of the axle using the large knife. First, create a cross.

13. Make two additional splits at a 45° angle. You can extend the splits by turning the knife until they are about 6" (15cm) deep.

14. Look for some small twigs and use them to spread the splits open.

15. Now you can place the waterwheel onto its axle. Push the wheel carefully into the axle so that there is a 45° piece of axle in each space between the paddle blades. This can be a bit tricky. The stability of this waterwheel shocks me every time. If you like or if it is necessary, you can further increase the stability by wrapping it with string behind and in front of the wheel.

16. Place the two forked branches for holding the axle in the water and put the waterwheel in the water. You can also use this technique to build a waterwheel that is attached at the center of the axle instead of at the front. To do this, take two axles and only split them crosswise. Then offset the axles by 45°, connect them to the waterwheel on both sides, and fasten the axle ends together with string.

This waterwheel doesn't only look great—it can be used to create power as well. For example, I once used a waterwheel to power a rotisserie grill. Let your imagination run wild. Trust yourself to create your own waterwheel-driven projects!

PROJECT

WINDMILL

The windmill reveals the secrets of the wind. It shows you how hard the wind is blowing and in which direction. Windmills can be used to generate electricity as well as power pumps or machines. I like the idea of making wind power visible.

In my first book, *Crafting with the Pocket Knife*, I explained how to whittle a windmill. Thanks to its low weight, this feather windmill works with even very little wind. But this also has disadvantages. First, it's very hard to find suitable feathers for this windmill. Also, it must be made very precisely so that the feathers do not constantly fall out. Finally, feathers break easily. They are actually too weak for a children's toy.

In this book, I would like to show you how to make a windmill that faces the optimal wind direction on its own, is much more stable, and can be made almost anywhere with very easy-to-find materials. All you need are a few branches and a Swiss Army Knife. The dimensions provided here refer to the windmill in these instructions. You can build this kind of windmill however big or small you like. Use the material that you have available to you.

What You Need

For this windmill, you need a 20" (50cm) long stick with a diameter of 1" (2.5cm) to make the rotor blades and wind vane. For the stand, you need a long stick and for the cross bar at the top, you need about a ½" (1.5cm) thick and 16" (40cm) long stick. To allow the rotor blades and the top bar to move, you need a ³⁄₁₆" (5mm) thick stick and a small piece of an elder wood branch for the end of the axle. Finally, you need a bit of string and of course a Swiss Army Knife. Now you're ready to get started.

1. The total length of the propeller measures about 12" (30cm).

2. Cut a thick branch to this length and then split the branch with the Swiss Army Knife. If necessary, whittle a wooden wedge to split the branch (see page 191).

3. If you use hazel wood, as I do in the photo, the gap surface will be quite twisted in most cases.

4. Mark the middle of both halves respective to where the propellers will spin with two notches.

7. Saw a ⅛" (3mm) deep cut at the inner line of both blades.

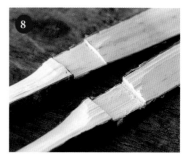

5. Whittle the areas of the split more heavily so that the beginning and the end of the stick have a 90° angle. This allows them to have a 45° angle in the wind. Whether or not this is the most ideal angle, I cannot say. In my tests, I was satisfied with the performance of this propeller.

6. Now lay the propeller blades at a right angle over each other and mark the point of intersection.

8. Split or whittle the groove for the overlapping area. If you were to place both pieces together now, you would get a good idea of how the final windmill would look.

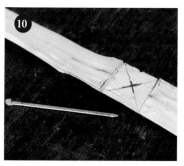

10. Mark the center of rotation for the propellers.

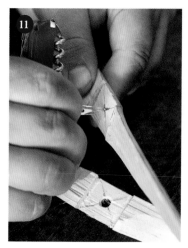

9. Whittle down the rounded sides of the propeller blades to be flat and ¹⁄₁₆"–⅛" (2–3mm) thick.

11. Make a ¼" (6mm) wide hole with the awl.

12. Connect the two pieces with string to create a finished propeller.

13. Now take the ½" (1.5cm) thick branch for the cross bar, and whittle the thick end to a small taper.

14. Take a 4"–6" (10-15cm) long remaining piece of the 1" (2.5cm) thick branch for the propeller.

15. Whittle two flat sheets for the wind vane.

16. Split the thin end of the cross bar about 4" (10cm) deep.

17. Insert the flat wood pieces for the wind vane and secure them with a tightly wound piece of string.

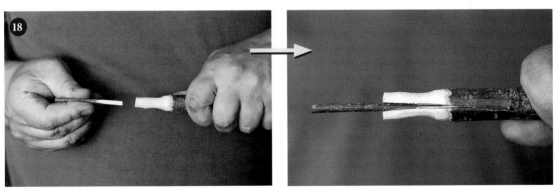

18. Make a slight split at the front of the cross bar and insert a flattened piece of the ³⁄₁₆" (5mm) thick stick in the opening.

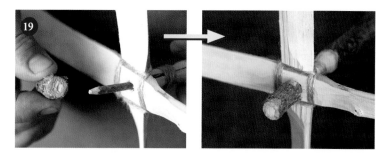

19. Fasten everything with a tightly wound piece of string. To make sure the string doesn't slip off, whittle a groove to catch and hold the string. Put the propeller on the axle and secure it with the piece of elder wood by pressing it into the center of the elder branch.

20. Find the center of gravity of the cross bar and make a hole. The rear section (between the hole and wind vane) should be considerably longer than the front section (between the hole and the propeller). If the ratio of these two is at least ⅔ to ⅓, the windmill should swivel very nicely in the wind.

21. Finally, whittle the bottom of the stand to a point so that you can easily insert it into the ground, and split the other end slightly. Then slide a thin, flattened piece of the ³⁄₁₆" (5mm) thick branch into the gap, as before, and attach a wrap string tightly around it.

22. Now all you have to do is connect your stand to the cross bar of your windmill and it's ready to go. Last but not least, you just need to wait for some wind. Until then, you can work on another project—for example, a wind machine!

PROJECT

ELDER WOOD PENCIL

In *The Swiss Army Knife Book*, I show how you can use small branches of willow and other trees to make charcoal for writing and drawing through carbonization in a vacuum. These charcoal pencils, however, are very fragile. Therefore, I wanted to create a kind of giant, sturdy pencil. The first tests were already very promising, so I kept working until I was completely satisfied. I think these pencils look great as well!

If you have wax crayons, it's very easy to make these in multiple colors. But if you're like me and want to make everything yourself from scratch, we'll need to dig a bit deeper into our bag of tricks.

What You Need

To make an elder wood pencil, you need an elder wood stick, a piece of candle or beeswax (if no wax is available, resin works as well), a piece of coal, a small can, and, of course, a Swiss Army Knife.

1. Saw the elder wood stick to your desired length.

2. Remove wood from the inside of the stick on one end with the corkscrew. The hole should be about 1½"–2½" (4–6cm) deep. Make a hole on the other end as well—it only needs to be ⅜"–¾" (1–2cm) deep.

3. Take a small piece of coal, hold it over the can, and crush it with your fingers.

4. Use a pestle to ground it into a fine powder. A good pencil requires very fine powder.

5. Now you need a bit of candle wax (paraffin or beeswax). Mix in as much wax as you have coal powder (by volume). I tend to add a bit more of the wax.

6. Now heat the mixture over a small flame or some embers until the wax is melted.

7. Stir the mixture and fill each side of the elder pencil, one by one, with the liquid wax.

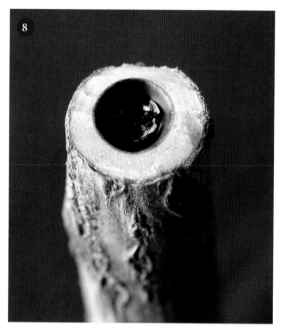

9. You can whittle the top part flat (where the hole isn't as deep).

8. Let the mixture cool. As it cools, the wax will shrink slightly. If you have some of the wax-coal mixture left over, you can reheat it and fill the remaining gaps. Let the mixture cool for at least 10 minutes.

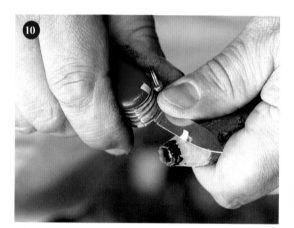

10. Carefully sharpen the bottom of the pencil. Be careful: as soon as you've whittled the wooden part of the pencil and reach the coal, you should switch to the fine-cutting technique. The coal needs to be whittled very carefully to prevent it from breaking off. Note: If you don't have a candle or candle pieces with you out in nature, you can create the lead for this pencil with resin. The pencil will be a bit harder and scratchier, but it still works quite well.

11. Now your elder wood pencil is finished—and nothing stands in your way of drawing a treasure map, writing a love letter, or sketching a masterpiece!

YO-YO

First and foremost: creating a yo-yo entirely out of natural materials is no simple task. In order for the yo-yo to work properly, the weight distribution needs to be perfect. This is difficult, but not impossible, and requires a lot of exact work. Those who successfully complete this challenge will be rewarded with a great toy that's loved by both kids and adults.

What You Need

To make a yo-yo, find a branch that's as round as possible, with a small pith. The branch should have a diameter of at least 1½" (4cm). You also need a piece of thin string, a thin branch for the axle, and a Swiss Army Knife.

1. Start with the two flywheels. Your first cut with the saw blade should be at a right angle. If you first use a pen to mark a line on the branch, this makes it easier to cut at a 90° angle. Don't cut completely through from one side. Instead, turn the branch after every few cuts. This prevents your cuts from going in the wrong direction. With this technique, the surface of the wood usually becomes rather bumpy, but it allows you to maintain the 90° angle more easily. The easiest way to smooth out the uneven surface is with the small blade. Check the angles of the cut from all sides. Open the awl, corkscrew, and multipurpose hook on the back of the Swiss Army Knife and place the Swiss Army Knife on the branch. The angle between the unfolded tools and the back of the knife should be almost exactly 90°.

2. Then, use a ballpoint pen to draw a second guideline to saw along. To do this, unfold the can opener tool and place the tip of the pen against the back of the Swiss Army Knife on the opposite side. This distance will create a flywheel that's about ½" (15mm) thick.

3. Saw with the same technique and whittle the surface smooth. Now you have the first half. Repeat this process to make the second half.

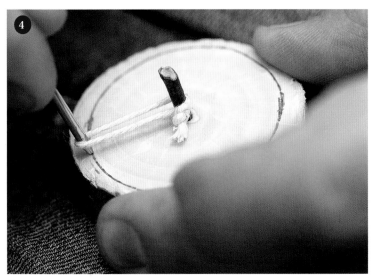

4. Once you've created both flywheels, draw a circle on both sides using an improvised compass to measure the outer contour. In this example, I made a compass out of a knotted piece of string and a branch that I placed in the middle of the wood.

5. Remove the outer rim using the large knife to make the circle as perfect as possible. You can use a flat, rough surface (like a concrete block) to perfect the discs and make sure they're the same size.

6. Then, use the reamer to make a hole for the axle in the wood.

7. Whittle the stick for the axle so that it fits. It should be a tight fit and stay in place.

8. Whittle a flat surface on the insides of both flywheels that will be facing each other, so that the string can wind and unwind freely.

10. Spin the disc so that the distance between both flywheels is ¼6" (2mm) and as even as possible all around. Then, cut off any excess part of the axle. Tie a knot in the string at about 32" (80cm) for your finger.

9. Cut off about 3' (1m) of string. Clamp the string between one of the flywheels and the axle, and press the second flywheel into the axle.

11. Now start your first attempt at your new yo-yo. Don't be frustrated if it doesn't work exactly how you wanted. I have noticed that a yo-yo will work differently depending on the type of string used. Try different strings, perfect the balance of your yo-yo, or work on your technique. Practice makes perfect!

PADDLE STEAMER

The idea behind this engine is ancient. During my Internet research for the "paddle steamer" project, I found a wonderful sketch from the fifteenth century by Mariano di Jacopo. He was an Italian engineer, artist, and public official of the city of Siena. Later, this engine and other similar engines were used for transporting goods on barges as well as for floating mills and sawmills.

I discovered such a paddle steamer in Walter Kraul's book *Earth, Water, Fire, and Air: Playful Explorations in the Four Elements*. The challenge for me was simplifying the project to be suitable for a Swiss Army Knife.

What You Need

For a paddle steamer, you need a large piece of bark or soft wood for the boat's hull and a 28" (70cm) long, straight hazel branch with a diameter of ¾" (2cm) for the paddles, axle bearings, and string eyelets. For the axle, you need a ⅜" (1cm) thick hazel branch. Then you need a thin stick, several feet (about a meter) of string, and a Swiss Army Knife.

These measurements apply to the boat in these instructions. The boat can also be built larger or smaller. Use the materials you have available to build the boat. Begin with the hull. Determine the maximum dimensions of the hull that can be made from the available material. In this case, the boat will be around 3½" (9cm) wide and 10" (25cm) long. Because the boat will go in both directions, I designed the hull symmetrically, so there is no bow or stern.

1. Saw and whittle a rectangle with the determined maximum dimensions. Then draw the hull shape.

2. Whittle it as needed.

3. Find the middle of the hull by using a blade of grass folded in half and mark this point.

4. Make a hole along the centerline ⅜" (1cm) from each side of the boat on both sides with the reamer.

5. Also make a hole at the top and bottom. Now your hull is finished.

6. Time to whittle the paddle wheels. The length of each paddle is two Swiss Army Knives long, so about 7⅛" (18cm). You need two branches of that size. Split both branches in half so that you have four pieces.

7. Whittle the separated side as flat as possible. Then, whittle some wood off the opposite side so that you're left with small ⁵⁄₃₂" (4mm) wide boards.

8. Mark the center of the boards using the blade of grass technique.

9. Saw a groove here through the middle and make it as wide as necessary.

10. Now you can put two boards together to make a cross.

11. Cut the branch for the axle to 10⅝" (27cm). Split the branch on one side to form a cross.

12. Place a paddle in the opening.

13. Secure the paddle with two tight wraps of string.

14. Split the opposite side at a 45° angle to the first, but don't insert the other paddle wheel just yet.

15. Now create four identical inserts: two axle brackets and two eyelets for holding the string. Saw off two pieces of the thick hazel branch about 2¾" (7cm) long and split them down the middle.

16. Whittle the back of them flat so you're left with four boards (this time about ³⁄₁₆" [5mm] thick).

17. Whittle the boards to a point on one side so that they fit into the hull of the boat.

18. The pieces that are put in the front and back of the boat's hull each receive a ⅛" (3mm) hole.

19. For the pieces on the sides of the hull, they should be given holes that are just big enough for the axle to easily pass through them.

20. Now you can insert the axle and the second blade panel.

21. Make a small hole with the awl just above the axle bearings for the locking pins.

22. Now you can thread the string through the eyelets in the boards at the front or back of the hull and tie it with a strangle knot to the axle.

23. Wrap ⁵⁄₃₂"–³⁄₁₆" (4–5mm) of string around the axle and tie a loop at the end of it.

24. Now the fun can begin! When you place the boat against the current, the line should unwind. If this is not the case, the string must be inserted through the eyelet at the other part of the hull. The boat moves away until the string is completely unwound. Then it begins to wind up on the other side and the boat moves against the current to you. The stronger the current, the faster your paddle steamer will move toward you. Once the boat has come back to you, you have to put the string through the eyelet on the other side of the boat, turn the boat, and the fun starts again!

Things That Sling, Shoot, and Fly

General Safety Rules for Shooting, Throwing, and Slinging Objects

➜ Never shoot at people or animals! Also never aim at people, even as a joke with no ammunition.

➜ Do not shoot at cars, windows, or other objects that can cause property damage.

➜ It is best to always shoot at a target or a suitable object such as a bale of hay, a cardboard box, a Styrofoam plate, a can, a balloon, a plastic bottle, or a juice box.

➜ Make sure your shooting range is safe even if you miss your target! For example, do not place your target on the fence next to your neighbor's yard.

➜ You must be able to see the projectile all the way to the target. That means only shoot what you can look at. If you shoot over a hilltop, into the forest, or over a house roof, you will not know if there is someone or something in the path of the projectile. It is best to block off the firing range with a tape or rope so that no one runs into the field of fire.

➜ If several people are shooting at the same time, a line must be drawn that can only be crossed if everyone has fired their ammunition and the person in charge gives the OK.

➜ Explain the safety rules to anyone who has not heard them yet.

NOTE: Be aware of all the laws concerning outdoor activities where you live, including laws about slingshots, bows, arrows, catapults, and boomerangs as well as plant and animal conservation laws. Children should always be supervised by adults if allowed to use or make slingshots and other shooting or throwing objects. When throwing or slinging an object, always know your target and what's behind it. Do not shoot at hard surfaces or at the surface of water. Objects may bounce off or ricochet and hit someone or something you had not intended to hit.

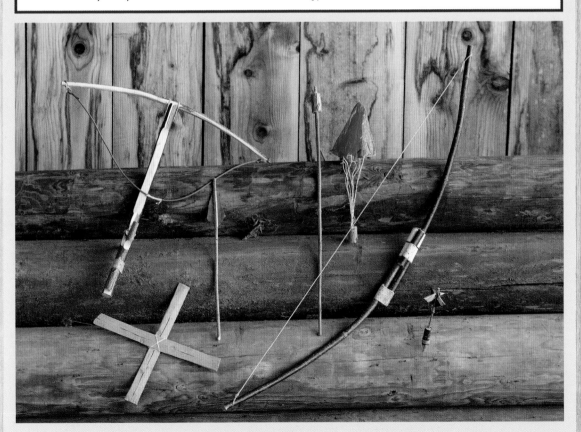

CROSSBOW

As inspiration for the participants at my carving workshops, I put some finished objects on a table. The crossbow is always one of the objects I include. Almost every time, I hear several children say, "I'm gonna make one like that today!" The crossbow fascinates not only children—parents are also amazed that you can whittle a crossbow with nothing more than a Swiss Army Knife.

What You Need

The crossbow consists of four parts: the shaft (with handle, arrow guide, and bow holder), the bow, the trigger, and the arrow holder. Of course, you will also need an arrow.

For the raw material, you only need two straight hazel sticks, each about 24" (60cm) long. The sticks should have a diameter of around 1¼" (3cm). In addition, you need a ⁵⁄₁₆"–³⁄₈" (8–10mm) thick stick for the arrow, a little bit of tape for the fletching, and string. I use parcel string made of hemp fibers; a plastic cord would work as well. The crossbow can be built larger or smaller than in the description below. It is more important that the proportions are the same.

The shaft is whittled from the thicker of the two sticks. The shaft should have the diameter of a bottle opener at the thick end. The length of the shaft is 21"–24" (55–60cm).

I built my crossbow entirely from hazel wood. Of course, you can also use other suitable types of wood for the bow: yew, locust, and elm wood are more resilient than hazel wood. Nevertheless, hazel works quite well, especially once the wood dries and the crossbow becomes harder after a week or two. At the same time, the arrows also dry out, making them lighter and able to fly faster and farther.

It takes a talented whittler and tinkerer to craft this crossbow. For example, I can't describe every last detail of building the trigger because it varies slightly each time it is built. Technical understanding and perseverance are therefore important prerequisites for the success of this project.

On the YouTube channel *feliximmler*, you can find a video (without sound) with the title "How to make a crossbow," where you can watch me build it.

1. Saw the stick about two Swiss Army Knife lengths from the end and stop at the middle of the stick.

2. Whittle a long notch into the stick from the thinner end.

3. Make two holes into the surface of the notch with the awl: one hole close to the 90° angle left by the saw cut, the other about ¾" (2cm) away.

4. Now use the small blade to carefully cut the bridge between the holes so that an elongated hole is created. Be careful with this step! With the saw and the small blade, widen the elongated hole so that the large screwdriver can fit across it.

5. Whittle a long indentation on the top of the shaft so the arrow will only make contact at the beginning and end.

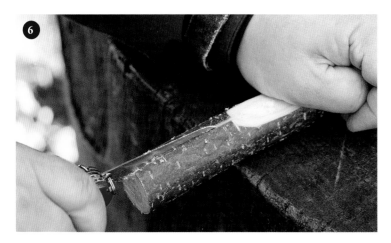

6. Now whittle a recess at both ends of the indentation to guide the arrow. To ensure that the notches are in alignment, you can use a piece of string to mark the center of each. Use the saw to make a center groove in each to make it easier to whittle the notch.

7. Finish the notch using the fine-cutting technique.

8. Make a horizontal groove as wide as possible on the front end of the shaft for later attaching the bow. Make the groove wide enough that the top and bottom parts of the branch still have a thickness of at least 5/32" (4mm).

9. Make several cuts with the saw to make the groove. Then, remove the remaining area with the small blade.

10. Use the saw diagonally to file down the groove and smooth it out (see the top left photo on page 196). Later, you will have to whittle the bow a little thinner in the middle so that it fits into this groove. Because this is the strongest part of the bow, it won't have any negative effects.

11. Using the awl, cut two holes through the underside of the shaft. The distance between the groove at the top and the holes should be the length of the awl.

12. Use the small blade and the saw to connect the adjacent holes to form an elongated hole. This will allow you to better secure the bow later by looping string through this hole multiple times.

13. Whittle the trigger. Use the remaining part of the shaft or bow to cut a piece of wood that's about the length of the Swiss Army Knife.

14. Split it lengthwise into two parts. Mark the head of the trigger on one of the halves. The trigger is slightly shorter due to the notch in the shaft.

15. Now use the saw to cut both sides from the marking to the middle.

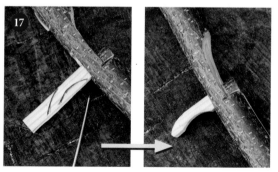

16. Remove the long sidepieces.

17. Use the small blade to whittle the trigger to fit into the elongated hole in the shaft. Make some markings and carefully whittle the shape of the finger grip in the trigger.

18. Next comes the bow. The length of the bow is about 24" (60cm) and the diameter of the branch is about 1" (2.5cm). Make sure the back of the bow stays intact when whittling! The back of the bow is the part of the crossbow facing away from you when firing. The back of the bow should never be whittled because cutting through a branch's growth ring creates a weak point and therefore increases the chances that it will snap. Even the bark should be left untouched.

Then whittle the bow belly. First, find the middle of the bow and mark all the way around. Starting from the middle, whittle the inner side of both bow arms. The inside of the bow's arms is known as the "bow belly." The bow belly is the part of the crossbow facing toward you when firing. First, leave 1¼" (3cm) of full thickness to the left and right of the middle of the branch. Then, taper the bow arms on the bow belly, starting from the middle to the bow ends. After this step, the thickness at the ends of the branch should be about ⅜" (1cm). Then taper the bow arms on the sides until the width is still around ½" (1.5cm) at the ends.

19. Finally, round off the whittled sections of the branch. Now hold the bow at the left and right ends and press the middle against your knee. This will give you a first impression of how much strength is required to bend your crossbow. If it requires a lot of strength to make the bow bend even slightly, whittle the bow arms on the inner side a bit more. The ends should bend with moderate effort. Then use the saw to cut notches at the ends of the bow arms. To do this, first saw the notches on the sides of the bow arms. Then angle the groove onto the bow belly at 45°.

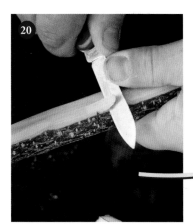

20. Now adjust the middle of the bow to match the front of the shaft so that the bow fits into the groove.

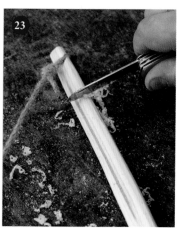

21. Now attach the shaft to the bow using the elongated hole you made before. Use string to keep it in place for now. If you only have thin string, use it to create a thicker cord. This provisional bow string should be about one and a half times as long as the bow.

22. If you pull on the bowstring, you can see if the bow arms bend evenly. Correct the ends of the bows until both sides bend evenly.

23. If one arm is too strong, whittle it thinner. If you only need to make a slight adjustment, don't whittle away the wood but scrape it off instead. This allows you to make very controlled adjustments without losing material (see "scraping," page 192).

24. Create and adjust the arrow holder. To attach the arrow holder to the shaft, you need to whittle a surface that slopes upward at the rear end of the shaft. The arrow holder makes sure that the trigger lever does not fall out of the groove. It aims the arrow and makes sure that the bowstring doesn't fly over the arrow when firing.

25. Split the branch that you are making the arrow holder from lengthwise. The length of the arrow holder should extend from the end of the shaft to the middle of the guide notch.

28. The arrow holder is attached to the end of the shaft with string.

26. Whittle a small recess into the arrow holder at the height of the notch in the shaft. This recess prevents the bowstring from flying over the arrow when firing.

27. Whittle a downward bending catch at the front of the arrow holder so that the arrow is not lifted out of the front notch when pressure is put on it from firing with your thumb.

29. Now the trigger and the bow strength need to be fine-tuned to work properly. This process can't be described in detail because there are many factors that may need to be corrected. Simply test and use your intuition and technical understanding until you're satisfied.

30. For arrows, we're using a straight $\frac{5}{16}$"–$\frac{3}{8}$" (8–10mm) thick hazel stick. The arrow should be as long as the distance between the trigger and the bow.

31. The fletching at the thinner end of the arrow can be improvised with a few pieces of tape stuck together and cut to size. Lastly, the tip of the arrow needs to be whittled to a point.

The general safety rules on page 57 apply to shooting with this crossbow.

To make this bow feel really Swiss, use an apple as your target like William Tell did. Just don't place the apple on a child's head—use a sturdy base like a tree trunk or a large rock.

PROJECT

TWO-STICK BOW

Most of us have probably made a simple bow and arrow out of a branch and string at some point as children. To increase the strength of such a bow, the two limbs must match in length and thickness. You need to work very carefully to prevent creating irreversible weak points when whittling, which can break the bow when used. Ideally, the entire bow works as one when the string is pulled: it bends evenly and force is spread equally across the length of the bow. To make this possible, the limbs of the bow need to be tapered from the middle of the bow where the grip is. For the two-stick bow, we will utilize the natural tapering of the branches and therefore we do not need to remove any of the wood.

What You Need

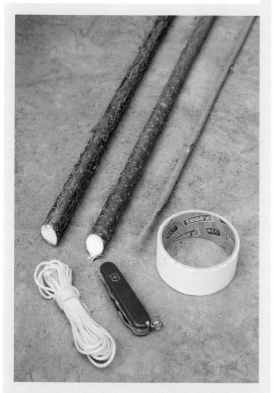

To make a two-stick bow, you need two equally strong and equally straight branches for the bow limbs, a thin branch for the arrow, tape for fletching the arrow, stable string, and a Swiss Army Knife. I mostly use hazel wood for my two-stick bow. Hazel bushes grow almost everywhere, and you can often find straight branches with few side branches. Of course, there's better wood out there to make a bow with, but those specimens are usually much harder to find.

1. The two branches for the limbs should measure about ¾" (2cm) at the thicker end. Cut a piece of branch about 28"–30" (70–75cm) long. This branch will have a natural taper of about ⅛"–³⁄₁₆" (3–5mm). Now place the cut branch next to the second branch and move it around to find the identical section of the second branch.

Cut this branch to the required length as well. Now you have two nearly identical bow limbs. If you place them on a table, the largest curve in the branch will lie flat. I try to use the natural curvature of the branches as much as possible, so that the branches are already bending slightly in the direction they will be pulled in when using the bow. If you use this natural bend the other way around, you may have a stronger bow but also a higher risk of the bow breaking.

2. The thick sides of the branches should overlap about 8"–10" (20–25cm) when put together. Look for a position where both overlapping branches seem even and the bow looks as symmetrical as possible. Mark the areas where the branches overlap.

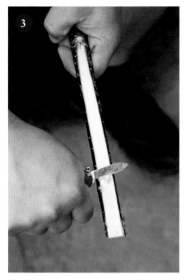

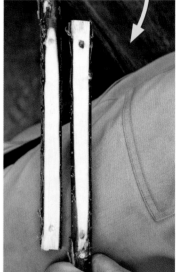

3. Whittle a sloping surface on both bow arms the length of the overlapping area and facing each other. Start very carefully and don't whittle past the markings you made—this would cause a weak point. You can whittle up to half of the material away from the thickest part of the branch.

4. On this surface, make two indents with the awl in the center of the first branch 1¼" (3cm) from the front and back.

5. To make sure the stones don't fall out of the indents, it is helpful to use some resin. Press a small, round pebble into the indents so that about half of it sticks out. (Instead of using string and pebbles, you could also stabilize the bow using tape and two nails. This is much easier but requires additional tools.)

Take the second bow limb and position the whittled surface against the first. Now press both whittled surfaces together. The two protruding stones will leave marks on the second branch. Use the awl to make two new indents on the second branch.

6. Tie both limbs together. Do this in the middle first before continuing to the two overlapping points. Then tie a hangman's knot on both ends of the grip.

8. Cut the string notches with your Swiss Army Knife saw about ⅜" (1cm) from the ends of the bow.

9. You can use a strong string or create a thicker cord if you only have thin string. Make an ordinary overhand loop at the end of the string.

7. The pebbles trick stops the limbs from moving side-to-side. If you prefer to shoot using an arrow rest and not off the back of your hand, feel free to attach a piece of branch as an arrow rest. The hangman's knot is used here as well.

10. The loop should be so big that it can just be placed over the end of the bow in the notch.

11. In my example, the string is 2¾"–4" (7–10cm) shorter than bow. Tie another tight loop with the same knot at the other end of the string.

12. You may have to open the second knot again and adjust it a little so the distance from string to bow is the size of your hand in a "thumbs up" position.

13. If the bow bends unevenly, you can straighten it slightly by pressing it on your knee.

16. Whittle a point at the thick end of the arrow.

15. For the arrow, I use a hazel branch that has naturally grown very straight. The lighter the arrow, the faster and farther it will fly with this bow. For this reason, I try to build the thinnest and lightest arrows possible. The arrow should be about as long as the distance between your chest and your pointer finger with your arms stretched out in front of you. I would not recommend making arrows shorter than around 20" (50cm). Your arrows should also be no thicker than ¼" (0.5cm) in diameter. These arrows have a diameter of ⁵⁄₁₆"–³⁄₈" (8–10mm) at their thickest end.

14. Follow this photo to get the string in and out. If the picture is not clear enough for you, you will find several videos about this on YouTube.

Always relax the bow when you are finished shooting. After you let the bow dry for two to three weeks, it will have more power than the freshly cut version.

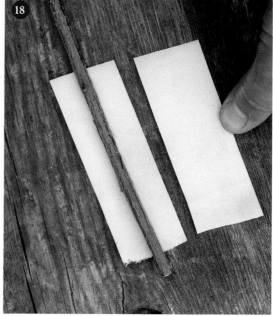

17. Saw a nock into the thin end of the arrow. I recommend stabilizing the arrow under your foot to do this because you need to saw toward yourself. If you slip, your shoe protects your foot.

18. The arrow will also get lighter after two to three weeks of drying and will fly farther. To make the arrow fly straighter, you can add fletching to the back of it. The easiest way to fletch an arrow is with tape. Cut two pieces of adhesive tape about 4" (10cm) long. Place a piece in the center of the rear part of arrow.

20. Now place the second strip of tape as evenly as possible over the first. Press the tape together with your fingers.

19. The adhesive tape should be aligned parallel to the notch.

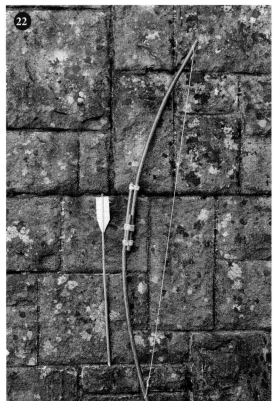

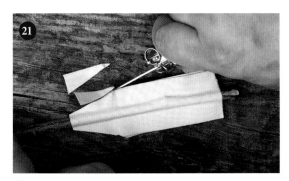

21. You can then use the scissors or a knife to cut the fletching to the desired shape.

22. Now your bow and arrow are finished. Please read the safety instructions on page 57 if you're not yet familiar with the rules for throwing and slinging projects.

On the *feliximmler* YouTube channel, you will find a video where you can watch me make this bow if you search for "two-stick bow." Have fun!

PROJECT

SWISS ARROW

At first glance, the Swiss arrow looks like a regular arrow that is too big for a bow. When you look closer, you'll see that there is a small notch behind the fletching. I will explain what this notch is for in the following instructions.

A few years ago, when I was looking for spear-thrower videos, I stumbled upon a video titled "Swiss Arrow." Since I'm Swiss, I wanted to find out what this was all about. The video fascinated me, and I attempted to recreate the arrow. Unfortunately, my attempts were unsuccessful. The arrow didn't fly any farther than when thrown normally with just my hand. I forgot about this project until, years later, a participant in a workshop told me that her cousin, who had grown up with her in northwest England, built such arrows and could use a string to hurl them through the air. He called these arrows "Dutch Arrows." Silvia could hardly remember any details, but she tried to build the prototype of such an arrow the same morning. Thank you, Silvia, for all your help!

What You Need

For this project, you need an arm's-length hazel wood branch, a piece of string, tape for the fletching, and of course a Swiss Army Knife.

The arrow can be built in different lengths. In the following instructions, I'm going to describe an arrow that I have been very pleased with. I used a 28" (70cm) long piece of hazel wood. The diameter was ½" (12mm) at the front and ⁵⁄₁₆" (8mm) at the back.

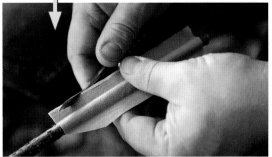

1. Whittle a point at the front thicker end. Then, make a 4¾" (12cm) long fletching with tape at the back.

2. Saw a notch facing the arrow tip two Swiss Army Knife lengths (about 7" [18cm]) from the thin end of the branch. Depending on the thickness of your string, you may need to make a second saw cut next to it.

3. With the small blade, open the notch a little and try to whittle it so that the string can hang comfortably when throwing the arrow. Warning: The notch should not be deeper than half of the diameter.

4. The string that you'll be using as a "sling" should be about 3' (1m) long. Make a knot at one end and melt it with a lighter.

7. My slinging technique is a bit strange but it works great for me: I aim with the end of the arrow and imagine hitting my goal with the back of the arrow. First, I wind up and begin the throwing movement.

5. The throwing technique: Similar to a spear-thrower, the Swiss arrow uses an extension of the arm to increase throwing power and acceleration of the arrow to the target. Whereas the spear-thrower is made of a piece of wood, the sling of a Swiss arrow is made of a piece of string with a knot at the end.

Place the end of the string in the notch and pull the knot onto the arrow shaft. Wrap the string once around the arrow and thread it behind the knot.

6. Tighten the string toward the front and wrap it one to two times around the arrow. Don't release the tension. Wrap the other end of the string around your hand or finger, and hold the point of the arrow with your throwing hand.

8. As soon as the arrow is standing upright, I intuitively let go and finish the movement. I had to try many times before the arrow flew very far. You can find other online videos about slinging techniques under "Dutch arrow" or "Swiss arrow." Try it yourself and find which technique is right for you.

APPLE SLINGSHOT

A participant of a whittling workshop once told me about an apple slingshot that he used to fling rotten apples out of the orchard as a child. He later sent me a video showing his slingshot. I found the idea interesting, and I had lots of fun developing this new project.

Using the apple slingshot requires a bit of practice, especially if you're trying to hit a target and not just sling it as far as possible. The point at which the apple separates from the sling is always a bit different depending on the softness or ripeness of the fruit. Therefore, you must always be aware that the apple could fly in an unexpected direction. Sufficient space for trying out this project is a must! The slingshot also works with pears and other rotten fruit. Please only use fruit for this project that is truly rotten and no longer healthy to eat. Otherwise you would be wasting perfectly good food!

What You Need

To build an apple slingshot, you need a ¾"–1¼" (2–3cm) thick stick for the handle, a ³⁄₁₆" (5mm) thick small and sturdy branch for the spike, and 3' (1m) of strong string.

2. Whittle or saw a groove around the circumference about ⅜" (1cm) from the end. The string loop will later spin around this groove.

1. Shorten the stick to the length of your forearm.

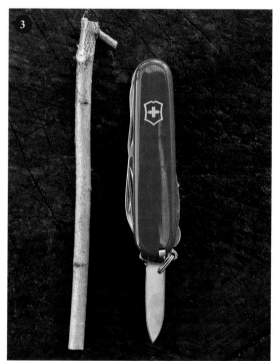

3. Now take the ³⁄₁₆" (5mm) thick small branch for the spike and cut it to approximately 4"–6" (10–15cm) long. To make sure the spike can't detach from the string, it's useful if the branch has a small side branch at the end.

4. Make a small hole on the opposite side ¾"–1¼" (2–3cm) from the end. Place a small piece of branch in the hole to act as an anti-slip mechanism for the apple.

5. When the apple separates from the spike due to centrifugal force, this locking pin will break or the apple will be soft enough that the wood will cut all the way through the apple. Whittle a point below the locking pin.

6. Now connect the handle and spike with the string. It is best to use a hangman's knot on the side of the spike with the small side branch (see step 5) and a cross knot on the side of the handle with the groove. You may choose to use a different type of knot if you wish. The string should be as long as the handle after being tied.

7. Now search for a rotten apple or a rotten pear, or another rotten fruit.

8. Remove the locking pin and press the spike through the fruit. Put the pin back into the hole and push the fruit back until it is against the locking pin. Now you can start!

9. Swing the handle so that the fruit circles over your head and aim at your target. When you're ready, you can fire your apple by making a similar movement to how you would throw a ball. The fruit will separate from the spike due to this acceleration and fly away. For me, these rotten apples fly a good 164'–230' (50–70m)—so much fun!

INDIAN BOW AND ARROW

Frank Egholm is a handicraft teacher and author from Denmark. I own quite a few of his whittling books. I was so impressed by one of his projects, so I asked him if I could include a modified version of his "Indian bow and arrow" in my new book. Thank you for your positive response, Frank! Frank learned about this project through a friend who spend his childhood in the Indian part of the Himalayas and built these kinds of bows. Hence the name "Indian bow and arrow."

I have achieved the best results with bows made of dogwood or cornelian cherry. There are certainly other types of hardwood that also provide good results. I also tried fresh hazel wood bows, but they weren't much fun to shoot. The performance of fresh hazel wood is limited, but a dry hazel branch is much more effective. However, in order to really have fun and be able to hit a target 23' (7m) away, I needed to use a hardwood bow.

What You Need

For this project you need an elder wood stick about ¾" (2cm) thick for the shaft (wooden grip) and a straight 3' (1m) long hardwood stick with two branches at the end for the bow. For the arrow you need a straight 4" (10cm) long, ⁵⁄₃₂"–³⁄₁₆" (4–5mm) thick hazel branch. You will also need the pin in the Swiss Army Knife, a piece of string, and a piece of cardboard or tape for the fletching.

I. Start with the elder wood shaft. Cut the shaft to about 20" (50cm) long. This is about the length of three unfolded Swiss Army Knives.

2. Use the awl to make a hole at the end of the shaft about 1½" (4cm) (about the length of the awl) from the edge. Enlarge the hole by twisting the saw inside it (see page 197). The hole should be large enough for the hardwood stick of the bow to fit through it. Then, make two additional holes on the other side of the shaft 4" (10cm) and 9" (23cm) from the end. They form the end points of the elongated hole that guides the bow. **Warning: All three holes in the shaft should be made in the same direction!**

4. Use the small knife on the outside of a hole and press it into the branch until it splits. Turn the blade to lengthen the split to the other hole.

3. Now start making the elongated holes by whittling an area between the holes.

5. Do the same on the other side of the hole. Now you should be able to lift out the wood between the splits with the awl.

6. Do the same on the back of the branch.

7. Use the small knife to carefully enlarge the hole.

8. The bow should have one or two side branches at the end. This way, the bow cannot jump out of the guide.

9. To give the bow a little more room on the guide, you can cut off the bark at the end of the bow in front of the side branches.

10. Before inserting the bow into the shaft, I recommend pre-bending it. Look for a round tree trunk with a diameter of about 12" (30cm) and bend the hardwood slightly beyond 180° around it. This helps the wood bend better and prevents the branch from breaking. Now you can use the bow. First insert the thinner end with the side branches into the elongated hole.

11. Insert the thicker arch end through the other hole only after the previous step.

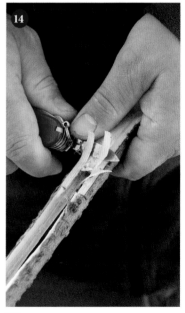

12. In the following steps, you'll whittle a ramp into the shaft to guide the arrow. Saw a ⅜" (1cm) deep cut ¾"–1¼" (2–3cm) away from the end of the elongated hole.

13. Split off a ⅜" (1cm) thick piece of the shaft.

14. Use the fine-cutting technique to whittle this area flat.

15. Remove the wood pulp.

16. Lay the saw flat against the surface and saw a fraction of an inch deep into the shaft in the direction of the elongated hole. Later, you will use this groove to insert the arrow's fletching.

17. Whittle the arrow. For the fletching of the arrow, thin cardboard or a piece of thin plastic works well. Cut the wings to the dimensions you prefer.

18. Now, split the thin side of the arrow slightly deeper than the length of your wing and insert the fletching.

19. Tie the sides together with string.

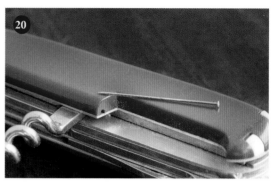

20. Take out the pin from your Swiss Army Knife. If you don't have a pin, you can use a thin nail, a piece of wire, a paper clip, or anything that is thin, hard, and sharp.

21. Now split the thick side of the arrow shaft an inch or so deep, as with the wing, and push the pin in with the tip outward.

22. Use string to hold both sides of the split together.

23. It takes a bit of practice to shoot the bow. I like to use Styrofoam as a target. The arrow also sticks nicely in wood. When shooting with the bow, follow the usual safety rules found on page 57. Whether you're Indian, Swiss, or something else, I think everyone can enjoy shooting a bow at an inflated balloon or other target.

SLINGSHOT TUBE

In 2014, Stefan Hinkelmann published a video entitled "Kondom des Grauens" ("Condom of Horror") on his YouTube channel *Survival Deutschland* (*Survival Germany*). With a condom, a plastic bottle cap, and a kebab skewer, he built a slingshot that became the inspiration for this project.

What You Need

For the slingshot tube, you need a piece of elder wood 3¼"–4" (8–10cm) long with a diameter of 1½" (3cm) or more. You also need some string, two strong rubber bands, and a Swiss Army Knife.

For the arrow, you need a straight stick of hazel wood as long as the distance between your chest and your pointer finger with your arms stretched out in front of you. Finally, you need a nail, the Swiss Army Knife pin, or a piece of thin wire for the point of the arrow, and some tape for fletching.

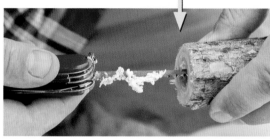

1. Start with the tube. Remove the pulp of the piece of elder wood with the corkscrew and the saw. Make the hole wide enough to be able to turn the saw inside it.

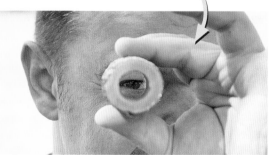

2. Now you can continue to whittle the hole with the large and small knives until it has a diameter of ¾" (2cm).

3. Whittle some bark away from the edges.

4. Saw a groove around the tube one-third of the way from the front.

5. Now take a thick piece of string or twist some string into a cord and form a tight loop.

6. Connect the rubber bands to the loop as shown in the pictures, so that you have a rubber band on both sides of the loop. This creates the tension element made of two rubber bands and a middle section made of string, which will later hold the arrow in place.

7. Now attach the two rubber bands to the tube by first looping string through the rubber bands and tightening them around the groove in the tube.

8. The sling is finished. Now you can make the arrow.

9. Carefully saw a groove through the thin side of the arrow with the saw blade. This groove will allow it to be held by the string. Because this requires you to saw against the body, I recommend holding the stick in place with your foot. The shoe protects your foot in case you slip.

10. Now whittle a point into the other end of the arrow.

11. With two pieces of tape laid on top of each other as evenly as possible, create the arrow fletching.

12. Use the scissors of the knife to cut the fletching to the right shape. It must still be thin enough to pass through the tube without friction.

13. Now your tube slingshot is finished. Please follow the safety rules on page 57 when shooting. I hope you have a lot of fun with this unique tube slingshot.

PROJECT

DART ARROW

I had never seen a self-whittled wooden dart arrow before I attempted this project. After the first few tests, I had so much fun with it that I decided to further develop it and introduce it here in this book.

A dart arrow can be built in different sizes. The following instructions are for an approximately 6" (16cm) long dart arrow. This size proved to be the best in my tests.

What You Need

To make a dart arrow, you need a Swiss Army Knife; a thin, straight branch that is ³⁄₁₆"–¼" (5–6mm) thick and 5⅛" (13cm) long for the shaft; a ¾" (2cm) thick, 4" (10cm) long branch of strong wood like cornelian cherry, dogwood, boxwood, or hornbeam for the grip; a 4"x4" (10x10cm) piece of waxy paper for the wings; and a nail or other small metal point for the tip.

A dart arrow consists of four parts: wings, arrow shaft, grip, and tip. Let's start with the tip. It's easiest to use a small nail for the tip. You can also use the pin from the Swiss Army Knife, but it would become bent very quickly. You can also make a great tip out of a paper clip or piece of wire. Simply sand one end down to a sharp point. If nothing else is available, you can also use a stone. If you are shooting at a rotted tree or any other soft object, a thorn (for example, from a hawthorn bush) can also work as a point.

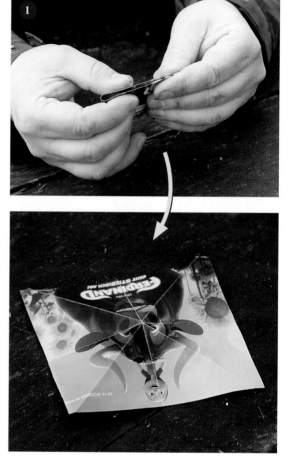

I. For the wings, you need a piece of thick paper or thin cardboard. If the paper is coated like the kind in a glossy magazine, it will be less susceptible to moisture. Wrapping paper also works well. Fold the paper in half twice. Then unfold it and fold it diagonally in one direction; unfold it and fold it diagonally in the other direction. When the paper is now unfolded, you should see creases that form a star.

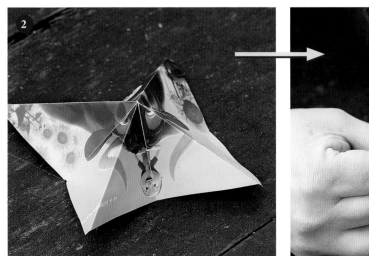

2. Then shape the paper until four wings appear.

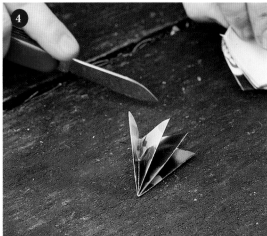

4. Then, open up the wings again.

3. Fold the four wings over each other and cut a piece of the open side off to form a triangle.

5. Now for the shaft: Split the branch crosswise at its thinner end so that the wings can fit inside. I like making the split deep enough to be able to tie string in front of, as well as behind, the wings.

6. Finally, the grip: In a store-bought dart arrow, the handle makes up about 90% of the total weight. Cut off a 2¾" (7cm) long piece from the branch. This is about the length of the large knife.

7. Whittle a point into the grip and split it.

8. Take the nail that you will use for the point, place it between the two halves, and press firmly together. Now you have impressions of the nail in the right place.

9. Use the small blade to work with the core of both halves. Whittle a groove into both halves.

10. Create an indent where the nail will sit that will allow the two halves to come together evenly.

11. On the other side, where the shaft will sit, whittle an indent about ¾" (2cm) deep for both halves.

12. Bring everything together and secure it with two tightly wound pieces of string. Now the dart arrow is finished. Bravo! But be careful: The safety rules on page 57 apply here as well, just like with all slinging, throwing, and shooting projects.

PARACHUTE

The idea for building a parachute came from my photographer, Matthew Worden. As a child, he had a toy parachute that he could shoot in the air with a toy rocket. It would open in mid-air and float gently back to the ground. His idea was to use the stone slingshot or bow and arrow to fire it into the air. So, he built a prototype parachute with all the trimmings. Unfortunately, this design (as with many prototypes) did not work right away, so we continued to work on it. Finally, we came across a simple solution that we were happy with.

You can read how to build a proper bow for this parachute on page 66.

What You Need

For the arrow, you need a straight young hazel wood branch. You will also need a piece of elder wood with a diameter of 1" (2.5cm) for the arrow as well as the parachute. For the parachute, you will also need a plastic bag (for example, a dog waste bag), a few feet of thin string, and a lighter.

1. Saw a marking cut on the elder branch one length of the Swiss Army Knife from the end.

2. Place the saw on the marking and cut at a 45° angle slightly past the center of the branch.

3. Place the saw in the middle of the branch, and cut through the branch.

4. Use the splitting technique to remove a triangle where you made your 45° cut.

5. Saw through the branch where you made your initial marking.

6. Now you have two pieces of wood about 1¾" (4.5cm) long: one with a notch and one without.

7. Use the awl and corkscrew to remove the wood from each piece.

8. Take the hazel wood branch for the arrow and whittle down the first 4" (10cm) so that it gets stuck into the elder wood piece without the notch and won't come apart.

9. Now cut the hazel branch 1¼" (3cm) before the elder wood piece. The second piece (the one with the notch) must be placed over the protruding tip without getting stuck. It's very important that the second piece has enough room to move around.

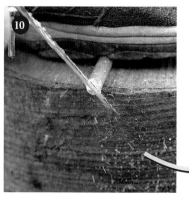
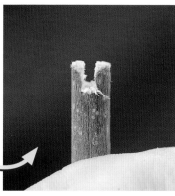

10. Saw a notch on the other side of the arrow that will connect with the bowstring when shooting.

11. I used a dog waste bag for the parachute. Fold the bag in half from the open end down to the bottom.

12. Fold a corner from the bottom across the fold you just created to make a triangle with a 45° angle. Fold the triangle in half again to create a 22.5° angle.

13. Use the knife or scissors and cut the plastic on the bottom, open side to create an isosceles triangle.

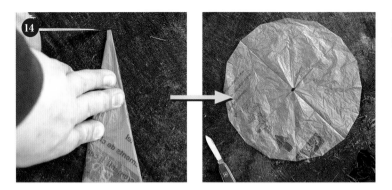

14. Also cut off a small part of the tip of the triangle and unfold the bag.

15. Take your Swiss Army Knife pin and stick it pinhead first into the core of the small branch.

16. Now heat the tip of the pin with the lighter. Then, burn a hole with the pin at every second fold in the plastic so that you have eight holes for threading the string.

17. The eight thin strings should be about 1.5 times as long as the diameter of the parachute.

18. Thread the strings through the holes and tie them off. If you have tape on hand, it is a good idea to use it at the places where you burned the holes to prevent tearing.

19. Place a heavy, round object (like a rock) in the middle of the parachute, and tighten all the lines.

20. Tie a knot at the end of the strings.

21. Cut off the remaining strings.

22. Press the knot into the hole of the elder wood piece with the notch you made earlier.

23. Now the parachute is finished.

24. To get the parachute onto the arrow, hold the parachute at the top with one hand and use the other hand to flatten it.

25. Now place the middle of the parachute across the arrow, and place the elder wood piece with the notch over it to hold it in place.

26. Shoot the arrow upward. The arrow will stop at the highest point, and because the heavy part of the arrow is always in front, it will eventually turn so the heavy part points to the ground. When this happens, the loose elder wood piece will separate from the arrow, opening the parachute.

In about six of ten attempts, the parachute opened at a height of 49'-66' (15-20m) and slowly floated back to the ground. In the other four attempts, the parachute remained attached to the arrow and didn't open for one reason or another.

The parachute project is for tinkerers and people who don't stick their heads in the sand at the first failed attempt. When the project does work, that makes it all the more satisfying. Matthew and I enjoyed this project and were reminded of Neil Armstrong: "A small step for mankind, but one giant leap for two people!"

BOOMERANG

When I was about ten years old, I made my first boomerang in shop class. It had four wings with a hole in the middle. Back then, I cut the boomerang out of a plywood board with a jigsaw and worked out the contours with a rasp and sandpaper. I can still remember throwing it for the first time on the soccer field next to the school. Our teacher almost went crazy because we had not followed his instructions and threw our boomerangs all at the same time instead of one after the other. He had warned us before that throwing several boomerangs at the same time was extremely dangerous.

Because I could envision making such a boomerang with a Swiss Army Knife and because I already had positive experiences with this type of boomerang design, I decided to try it out a few years ago. And so, this boomerang project was born. In this chapter, I will show you how to make a four-wing boomerang out of birch wood. In my experience, birch wood has very little spiral growth if you split it lengthwise. Whenever I tried other wood like hazelnut or ash, the spiral growth had negative effects on the final product. The spiral growth made it almost impossible to whittle the bottom of the boomerang flat. I always got the best results when the bottom of the boomerang was flat.

What You Need

To complete this project, you need a straight branch with as few side branches as possible approximately 16"–20" (40–50cm) long, a piece of string, a Swiss Army Knife, and two wedges to split the branch with.

The branch should have a diameter of 1⅜"–1⅝" (3.5–4cm), which is about the same length as the Swiss Army Knife awl.

1. Carefully split the branch. How to do this is described in the section "Splitting with homemade wooden wedges" on page 191.

2. Smooth the split surfaces and cut the branches (i.e., the "wings") to the length of approximately 12¾" (32cm). This is the length of two Swiss Army knives with the large blade extended.

3. Split and then whittle away any excess material on the insides of branch halves until you have two boards, each ³⁄₁₆″–¼″ (5–6mm) thick.

4. Use a pen to mark contours on the wood as shown here and begin whittling.

5. To allow the wings to hook into each other, create a recess on the top of one of the wings and on the bottom of the other wing, like a log house. Place the wings on top of each other in the right position and mark where they cross from the top and bottom.

6. Looking at the end of each wing from the side, it should resemble an airplane wing.

7. Whittle with the saw on the markings to about half the thickness of the wood.

8. Place the saw cut ¹⁄₆₄"–¹⁄₃₂" (0.5–1mm) closer to the middle than the marking. The goal is that the wings can be stuck together and won't come apart. Whittling the thin side a bit narrower if needed is quick and easy. Carefully remove the wood between both cuts. There are many methods of doing this, and all of them are suitable. One approach is to use the fine-cutting technique to whittle them out. Another method is sawing a groove every ¹⁄₁₆"–¹⁄₈" (2–3mm) and then breaking away the ridges by twisting the saw. By using the saw as a file, you can smooth the bottom of the recess.

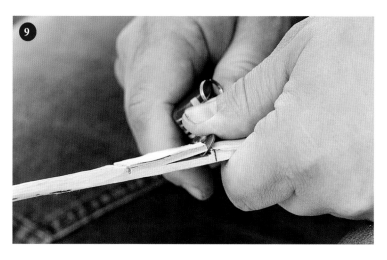

9. The third approach is the quickest but also the riskiest: place the large blade into the groove and turn it.

10. This will split off the wood you want to remove. Afterwards, you need to whittle away some excess.

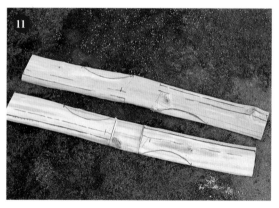

11. Mark the indentation up to the middle of each wing and cut these away. These indentations serve to shift the center of gravity toward the ends of the wings, making the boomerang stronger and allowing it to spin longer.

12. Place the wings together and secure them with string, forming an X across the center. Of course, you can also use wood glue.

13. Finally, round off the corners a bit to prevent chipping during hard landings.

14. Now the boomerang is finished.

15. Don't get discouraged if the boomerang doesn't come back to you on your first try. First try to improve your throwing technique: throwing power, rotation, wind direction, angle, and direction (upward or straight ahead) are all factors that influence how the boomerang flies and whether it comes back or not. You can also change a lot on the boomerang itself (e.g., whittling away more material). To describe all of these in detail would be too much for this book. When you whittle a boomerang, you shouldn't expect to be able to stay in the same spot and catch it on your first throw. Of course, I have been able to achieve this with some boomerangs, but I also find it fascinating when my boomerang flies in a semicircle.

By the way, my shop teacher was absolutely right! Make sure that you have enough space to throw and that no other people or animals are within the range of your boomerang. After all, boomerangs were used by native Australians as hunting weapons!

SHINGLE ARROW

When I was searching for new projects for this book, a few older people told me about arrows they made from shingles cut in the shape of a spatula, which they launched over meadows and fields with a type of whip. Obtaining precise information about how these shingle arrows were made was difficult because most only had vague memories about them. One person who could explain in detail how to whittle such an arrow was Martin Müller from Stalden in the canton of Obwalden, Switzerland. Martin and his brother Andy are known as the "Feuerbrüder Müller" ("Müller fire brothers") and are the ultimate Swiss fire experts. Many thanks, Martin, for your photos and valuable tips!

Because I want this book to only include materials that you can find in nature, I did not use actual wooden shingles for this project. Instead, I whittled my own arrows out of shattered wood from a fallen tree trunk.

When it comes to shingle arrows, it's important to understand how they work. The heavy part of the arrow flies ahead. This is why our shingle arrow must have more mass in the front at the tip than in the rear at the tail. The balance point needs to therefore be closer to the front than to the rear. Because the tail end has more surface area than the tip, it has to be whittled very thin, leaving much more material in the tip. The notch that the cord of the slingshot hangs in should be slightly before the balance point, toward the tip. Both the size and the shape of the shingle arrow can vary. In the following instructions, I will show you how to make a shingle arrow that worked well in my experiments.

What You Need

For a single arrow, you need a flat piece of wood (this is what the shingle arrow is made from), a branch, some string for slinging the arrow, and a Swiss Army Knife.

1. Look for a board from a broken tree trunk that is about 20" (50cm) long, at least 1½" (4cm) wide, and at least ⅜" (1cm) thick.

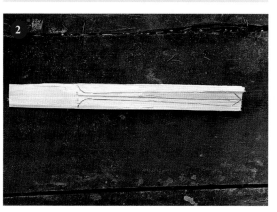

2. Whittle the top and bottom of it flat enough to be able to draw the shape of the arrow on it. The arrow should be about 17¾" (45cm) long and the tail should take up about a third of the length.

3. Whittle the wood to create the arrow's shape. Always whittle from the outside in, or from the thick area to the thin area.

4. Once you're happy with the shape of the arrow, begin to work on its thickness. Leave the first 3¼"–4" (8–10cm) at the tip untouched. Then whittle the arrow thinner, making sure the tail is significantly thinner. I'm talking about ¹⁄₁₆"–⅛" (2–3mm) here! Round off any sharp edges. This makes the arrow less susceptible to a rough impact (less chipping).

5. Use the back of the blade to determine where the arrow's balance point is and mark it.

6. Draw a notch on the arrow. The bottom of the notch should be slightly in front of the balance point, toward the tip. Use the saw and the small blade to cut out the notch.

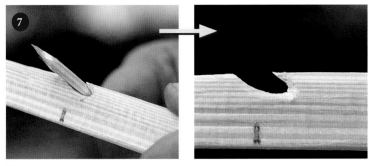

7. It's best if you smooth out the notch with a file so the string can move freely and won't get caught on any jagged edges. I use a whittled piece of wood to round out and smooth out the notch.

8. After the arrow is finished, you just have to make the sling. For this, use a stick about arm's length (⅝" [1.5cm] thick). Carve a notch at the end of the stick so that the string won't slide off. Tie the string tightly. A strangle knot is best for this.

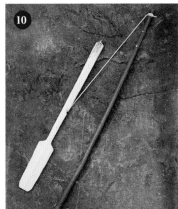

9. At the other end of the string, make an overhand knot with two loops. If you want, you can melt the knot with a lighter. The string should be half as long as the stick. Hang the knot in the notch in the shingle arrow.

10. Now the shingle arrow is finished. Please use the same safety rules (page 57) as shooting a bow and arrow.

11. When you first test your shingle arrow, it is very important that you make sure you have enough room in all directions. It takes a bit of practice to get the arrow to fly in the right direction.

PROJECT

STRING CATAPULT

I knew when I was gathering ideas for this book that I wanted to include instructions on how to build a catapult. However, it took some time until I knew what kind of catapult it should be. It would probably have been easy to build a catapult with exercise bands or rubber bands, but I wanted to have a catapult that could be made with the simplest materials.

What You Need

For this catapult, you need four sticks, string, and, of course, a Swiss Army Knife. The dimensions of the catapult depend on the length of the throwing arm. I decided to use a throwing arm that was about 12" (30cm) long. I used hazel wood for all parts of this catapult. You can use other types of wood just as well.

1. For the frame, you need two 1"–1¼" (2.5–3cm) thick, approximately 24" (60cm) long hazel sticks. Whittle them to a point on one side.

2. The cross bar, which acts as a separator, should be made from a stick that has the same thickness but is half as long as the side sticks—about 12" (30cm). Since the separator also serves as the stopper, you need to saw a V-shape indentation into both ends 3. This will prevent the cross bar from flying out when the throwing arm hits it.

3. Insert about one-third of the first side stick into the ground. Then, place the cross bar with the indentation against the first side stick and place the second side stick to fit into the indentation on the other side.

4. Now tie the string, depending on its thickness, five to ten times around both side sticks. The catapult will work with many types of string. I have tried paracord, hemp cord, and packing string. In the pictures, I'm using polypropylene packing string. I have gotten very good results with it.

5. Now let's make the throwing arm. The stick for this can be a bit thinner than both side sticks. The length of the throwing arm should be twice the distance between the string and the ground. To determine the correct length of the throwing arm, use a small branch. Mark the middle of the throwing arm with a small notch.

6. Now whittle a small recess ¾" (2cm) near the end of the stick using the awl and small blade, which will later be used to hold your catapult's ammunition.

7. I use a small, fingernail-sized stone as ammunition—this is how big the recess should be.

8. Now place the throwing arm between the strings. The center marking on the throwing arm should line up with the height of the string. Now turn the throwing arm in the opposite direction of fire. In order to pass over the cross bar, you need to tilt the throwing arm.

9. Turn the throwing arm until the twisted cord begins to become very tight. The amount of strength needed to turn the stick is the amount of energy your catapult will have. Don't overdo it at first. Do a couple test shots when the string is not too tight. You can always make it tighter. Remember: Pride goes before a fall! I have accidentally broken a side stick or ripped the string before. Have fun with your string catapult! You can really sling to your heart's desire.

SLINGSHOT

I described making a slingshot in my first book, *Crafting with the Pocket Knife*. Back then, I used exercise bands and string to build it. Because my goal is to create projects with natural materials or those that are very easily available, I will show you how to make a simple version of this slingshot with everyday rubber bands. The size and strength of the rubber bands doesn't really matter: short bands can be looped together to be made longer, and multiple thin bands (with little slinging power) can be used together to increase firepower. You don't need any string for this project. All connections are made with a lark's head knot.

What You Need

To build a slingshot, you need a forked branch, a small piece of leather, a few rubber bands, and a Swiss Army Knife. The basic structure of the slingshot is the forked branch. Ideally, the forks should be at a 50° angle. The forks should not be thinner than around ½" (1.2cm).

I. Cut both forks to about 4" (10cm) long. If the forks are too long, the resistance becomes so strong that kids cannot use the slingshot. A handle length of about 3" (8cm) is usually enough. Make a groove ⅜" (1cm) below the end of each of the forks with the saw.

2. Whittle the groove wide enough for the rubber band to fit in it. You don't want the rubber band to slide off the branch. It can be difficult to widen the groove because the other fork might be in the way. The best thing to do is to support the end of the fork and your carving hand on a stable base. This will help you make controlled cuts.

3. You are finished when the groove is ⅟₃₂" (1mm) deep.

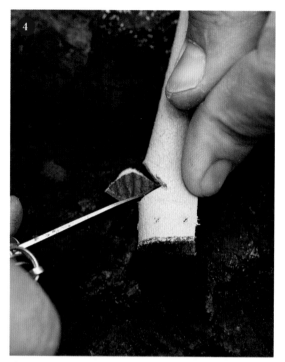

4. A piece of strong leather serves as an ammunition holder. Fold the leather lengthwise and cut out a triangle ⅜" (1cm) from the edge.

5. When you unfold the leather, you'll have two holes.

6. Loop the desired number of rubber bands together. For example, in the photo I used two rubber bands on each side.

7. Loop the rubber bands the same way through the holes in the ammunition holder and pull the knots tight.

8. Now you just need to loop the ends of the rubber bands around the forks in the slingshot. Do this with the lark's head knot. Use your thumb and index finger and place one side of the rubber band through the opening and over the other. Now you have "loops" around your thumb and index finger.

9. Place these loops over each other, pull your thumb out, and place the loops over your index finger. Pull out your index finger and place both loops over the end of the fork. Do the same for the other side of the ammunition holder. Now carefully pull the knots so that they are tight around the ends of the forks. Now your slingshot is ready to go. And so are you if you follow the safety rules on page 57.

10. You're ready to sling to your heart's content. It's especially fun to compete with your friends and see who can hit the tin can or the tree trunk first. Who will get ten hits first? Who will be the slingshot king or queen? Nice shot!

PS: You can compete with all slinging, throwing, and shooting projects using the "handicap rule." Experienced shooters must score more with the same shots than those with little to no experience. Younger competitors are allowed to stand closer to the goal and/or need less successful shots to win. Be inventive, give everyone a chance, and follow the Olympic mentality: participating is more important than winning!

THREE-SHOT RUBBER BAND GUN

Who hasn't joked around at school or in the office with a rubber band? As a child, together with my classmate, we had the glorious idea of seeing if we could shoot one at the blackboard from our desk during class. It worked, but of course we also had to clean the blackboard for a week afterwards. Hitting colleagues' computer screens in the office—you gotta have fun, even at work. Sometimes when I was firing the rubber band it hit my thumb: "Ouch!" That's why I often stretched the rubber band over a ruler. I was able to aim a lot better than if I had stretched it over the tip of my thumb. As a child, I also built a rubber band gun with a clothespin as a trigger. Of course, there are toys that are more educational than a rubber band gun. But it was still so much fun. Especially if you can fire three shots in a row.

What You Need

The three-shot rubber band gun consists of three parts: tube (barrel), trigger, and grip. For this project, you need a straight hazel stick approximately 32" (80cm) long with a diameter of about ¾"–1" (2–2.5cm). Out of this you will whittle the tube, trigger, and grip. You will also need a small branch for the trigger axle and the retraction bolt, which also serves as a gun sight. To attach the handle, you need some string and, of course, rubber bands for the trigger as well as for ammunition.

1. For the tube, cut the branch to the length of four Swiss Army knives laid back to back, about 14" (36cm).

2. Make a hole that is one Swiss Army Knife length from the branch's thickest end.

3. Split the branch toward the hole to make a large groove in the branch the width of the hole.

4. Use the small blade to whittle more wood away until the groove has the right width.

5. Once the gap has reached a certain size, it becomes easier to widen the groove. You are finished when the groove is approximately 5/16" (8mm) wide.

6. Use the awl to create a sideways hole 1" (2.5cm) above the bottom of the existing groove.

7. Make another hole at the front end of the tube in line with the groove. It should be deep enough for the awl to fit inside it.

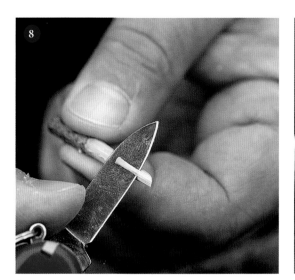

8. Now whittle a small branch to a point and hammer it carefully into the hole you just made.

9. Cut the branch ⁵⁄₃₂" (4mm) above the tube. This is the retraction bolt from which the rubber band is stretched and also the sight for aiming.

10. Now make the trigger. Cut off a piece of branch as long as the Swiss Army Knife. Split off wood on both sides so that you're left with a ⁵⁄₁₆" (8mm) wide board.

11. Whittle this flat enough to fit into the groove.

12. Now make a hole 1" (2.5cm) from the end of the board through the middle of the wood.

13. If you take the bottom hook of the bottle opener in your Swiss Army Knife and insert it into the hole you just made, you can turn it to draw a perfect circle above it.

14. Whittle away the wood on the line you just made and smooth out the surface.

15. Draw the finger recess and the remaining contour of the trigger on the wood.

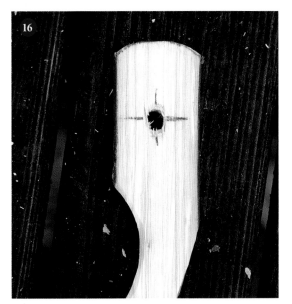

16. Whittle the trigger into the desired shape.

17. Now mark the positions of the notches where the rubber bands will later sit. The middle notch should be exactly horizontal to the hole. Draw two more notches to the left and right of the middle notch at about a 15° angle.

18. Saw the notches ⅛"–⁵⁄₃₂" (3–4mm) into the edge of the wood based on the lines.

19. Now comes the grip. The grip is about as long as two Swiss Army knives.

20. Whittle the upper third flat enough so that the grip fits into the groove in the tube.

21. And finally, the assembly. Insert the trigger into the groove in the tube and insert, if possible, a dry small branch through all three holes.

22. Try testing how far back you need to pull the trigger until the rear-most rubber band releases. This will help you determine the proper position and angle of the grip.

23. Hold the grip in place with some string.

24. Finally, saw a notch on the back of the trigger and on the bottom of the tube.

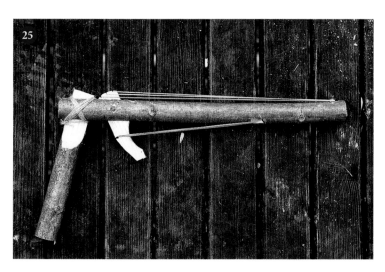

25. The counter-tension rubber bands will be hooked into these notches. Attach the rubber bands that you want to shoot as shown in the photo. These guns often require small adjustments to make the rubber bands fire at the right moment. Cut the notch holding the rubber band on the back of the trigger a bit deeper if it releases too early. Whittle a bit of wood away from the upper edges of the 5/32" (4mm) deep notches if a rubber band releases too late. Have fun with your three-shot rubber band gun!

Things That Whistle, Ring, and Rattle

REED FLUTE

I first saw a reed flute in the studio of a sound artist friend of mine, Stefan Philippi. He played so beautifully with this little flute that I got goose bumps. The tones and melodies that can come from a simple reed are unbelievable—as long as it has been properly made. The reed flute is one of my favorite projects.

What You Need

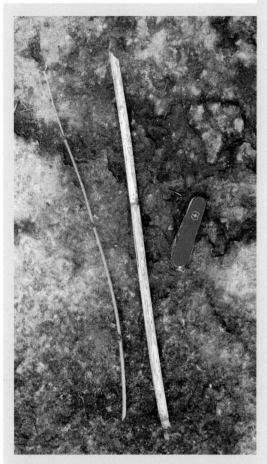

To make a reed flute, you need a dry reed stalk, a thin branch, a lighter, and a Swiss Army Knife with a razor-sharp small blade.

1. Look for an undamaged tubed segment of the reed. Remove the outer skin. The part that will eventually be used for the flute is open at the bottom.

2. The reed is blocked off at the top by a segmenting node. Because dry reeds are too brittle to shorten with the Swiss Army Knife saw, you need to use multiple cuts all around the reed slightly above this node. Burn the tips of the cut sections with the lighter. At the lower, open end, I shorten the tube with a diagonal cut (see step 1 photo).

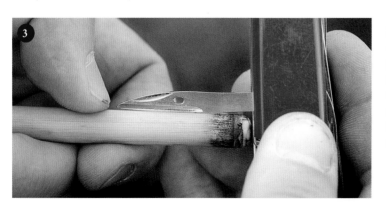

3. The way that the reed flute creates sound is the same basic principle as a clarinet or saxophone. The reed moves back and forth when blowing, causing the air column to vibrate. To whittle the vibrating reed into the reed pipe requires a sharp knife and absolute accuracy. Measure the length of one awl away from the node.

4. Use the small blade at an angle toward the node.

5. Use the fine-cutting technique to cut into the tube, curving the knife until the blade is parallel to the tube.

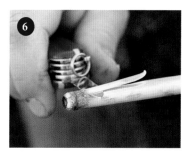

6. Carefully continue to elongate the cut up to the node. Be careful not to cut through the node! This cut is difficult because, among other things, the vibrating reed splits slightly at the start. If the split is short (as seen in the step 5 photo), it's usually not a problem. Otherwise, it is better if you take a new reed and start over.

7. In order for the cutout reed to vibrate when it is blown, it must protrude slightly when it is at rest. You can do this by weakening the surface of the vibrating reed by careful scraping (see page 192). Scrape from the node to ⅜" (1cm) before the end of the vibrating reed. This step takes a few minutes, especially with thick reeds, because the vibrating reed must be significantly thinner than the rest of the material. If you like, you can stick a thin chip under the vibrating reed when scraping. The vibrating reed will stick out with a bit of tension, making it easier to scrape.

8. Lift the vibrating reed slightly with the knife blade or with two fingers, and warm it up for two to three seconds with the lighter. Continue to hold the vibrating reed for a bit and let it cool down for a few seconds.

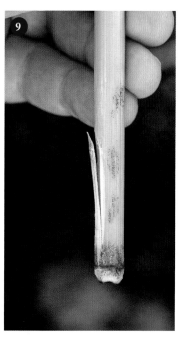

9. When you let go of the vibrating reed, it should stick out slightly.

Cleaning the Inside of the Tube

A look into a split reed shows that the inner wall is covered with a thin skin. This skin, when it sticks out, prevents the reed from making a sound. Therefore, you should scrape it out of the tube with a small stick. The stick should be longer than the flute so that the inner wall can be cleaned out all the way to the node. Now push the stick carefully into the reed and turn it until no more scraped material comes out of the opening. A non-airtight node can also be a reason why the flute does not make sound. Seal the node with chewing gum or resin, or press the tip of your tongue onto the opening while playing.

Try again to see if you can make a sound. Blow as hard as you can. If there is still no sound, the vibrating reed may still be too hard. Scrape more material off of the reed. But be careful: if the vibrating reed becomes too weak and can be squeezed without noticeable resistance, this flute is also unusable and you will have to start over.

10. See if you can make a sound. To do this, put the flute deep enough in your mouth so that the cut-out vibrating reed is completely behind your lips. Now close your mouth and blow into tube with varying intensities. If there is still no sound, you must clean the inside of the tube wall.

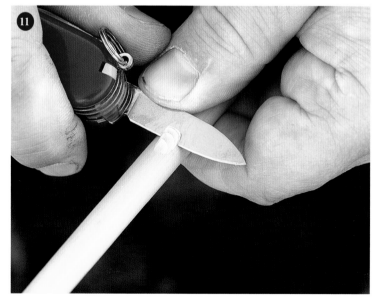

11. If the flute makes a sound, you can begin making the finger holes. Putting the holes in the right place to create a musical scale is very difficult. The distance and size of the holes could theoretically be calculated to do this, but that would go beyond the scope of this book. I'm happy if I can play a melody with some different tones on the flute.

Drilling the holes with the awl would split the flute, so the holes are cut. To do this, place the knife at the desired location and use the fine-cutting technique with several short cuts layer by layer.

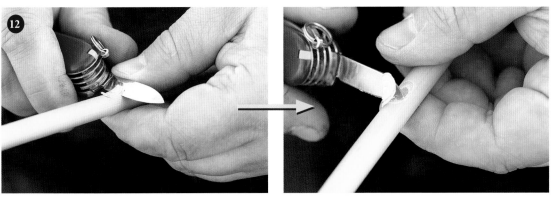

12. After three to four cuts, flip the flute and tap out the chips from the other side. Repeat this process until the wall is broken.

13. Use a lighter to burn off any remaining skin and protruding fibers to properly shape the hole. Repeat this process for each hole.

14. The number of holes is up to you and also depends on the length of the flute. I usually whittle four or five holes. You should start the bottom hole 1½" (4 cm) from the end of the flute. Then, make the next hole about ¾" (2cm) away from the last. Leave at least 2" (5cm) between the vibrating reed and the top hole so that you have enough space to grip all the holes with your fingers.

15. The final product could look something like this. With a little practice and imagination, you can create melodies to play again and again.

PROJECT

BALLOON SAXOPHONE

During my training as a nature educator at the Waldkinder Association (a club for children to learn about the natural world around them) in St. Gallen, Switzerland, we learned how to create instruments from natural materials in one of our courses. That's where I saw a balloon saxophone for the first time. I was fascinated by its simplicity and its warm, truly saxophone-like sound. During my research on this project, I came across building instructions on the Internet that explained it could be made with PVC pipes, a band saw, a drill, and a file. It was a challenge for me to create such an instrument using only natural materials and a Swiss Army Knife as the only tool. I tried several different ways of building it. They all worked, but most of them were very difficult to make. I am going to show you the easiest version in the following instructions.

What You Need

To make a balloon saxophone, you need a straight elder branch approximately 19" (50cm) long. The diameter should be ¾"–1¼" (2–3cm). For the best results, the branch should have at least ⅜" (1cm) of white pith inside. You will also need a short connector made from a branch about 1¼"–1½" (3–4cm) thick, some string, elastic bands or an old bicycle tube, a "pear-shaped" balloon, and a Swiss Army Knife.

2. Let's start with the main pipe. First remove the core from the wood. The cleaner the end of the pipe is, the better the instrument will sound! You can pull out the first 1½" (4cm) of the core on both sides with the corkscrew.

1. The length of the main pipe can vary. In this version, I will build a saxophone where the length of the main tube is about the length of four Swiss Army knives (14" [36cm]). The mouthpiece is about the length of one Swiss Army Knife. First, cut two pieces to these lengths from the elder wood branch.

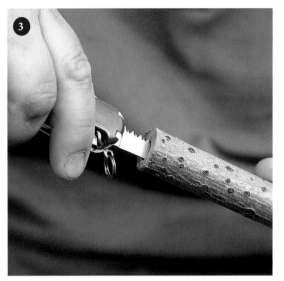

3. You can remove the next 1¼" (3cm) with the saw. It is important that you really try to get the soft core out and not just push it into the hole. Otherwise you will wind up with compressed core in the middle, which is almost impossible to remove without the help of additional tools.

If you have worked carefully with the saw, you will still have a little more than 8" (20cm) of core left that you have to get out somehow. The easiest way is with a long drill, a thick wire, or with a long screw. Because I want to avoid using such tools in this book, I am using a dry hardwood branch, which I cut diagonally at the front. I use this to try to pry out the rest of the core. This step is a bit tedious and takes a little patience, but it is absolutely possible to remove all of the core from the branch this way. In my experience, the core of a fresh branch is easier to remove than the core of a dry branch.

4. If you have created a continuous hole, you can use a thinner branch that still has a few side branches to "scrape" the walls like a chimney sweep.

5. Round off any sharp edges of the elder branch so that it won't damage the balloon you will use later. Do the same with the short elder branch for the mouthpiece.

PROJECT: Balloon Saxophone

6. Take the balloon and cut a small hole at the spot with the largest diameter. Now use two fingers to widen the opening of the balloon. Insert the mouthpiece into the balloon until the end of the mouthpiece is sticking out slightly.

7. Now put the hole in the balloon over the main tube and pull the balloon until the face of the mouthpiece is in contact with the main tube. The upper edge of the mouthpiece should form a straight line with the top of the main tube. The balloon should be slightly stretched over the main tube. If you now seal the bottom of the balloon by squeezing your fingers around the main tube and blow into the mouthpiece, you should already be able to hear a sound. If you don't hear any sound, blow harder into the pipe. If there is still no sound, try to clean the tube walls again, figure out the correct position of the mouthpiece or the correct tension for the balloon. Sometimes it also helps if you use the knife to whittle the hole at the top end a little wider so that the contact area of the balloon is reduced.

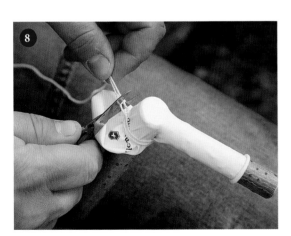

8. Once your instrument produces sound, tie the balloon airtight around the main tube with a piece of string. This string must be really tight so that absolutely no air can escape.

9. You can now cut off the rest of the balloon (below the string).

10. To stabilize the mouthpiece on the main pipe, I used a few rubber rings that I cut from an old bicycle tube with the Swiss Army Knife scissors and a branch about 2" (5cm) long, which serves as a connection. The branch can also be thicker than the main pipe. Now attach the connector to the mouthpiece and main pipe with the rubber rings. Do not place the rubber rings too close to the tight part of the balloon; you want to allow the balloon to expand and vibrate more easily. The vibration of the balloon causes the air column to vibrate. This is how the sound is created.

11. The position of the mouthpiece relative to the main tube influences the pitch. This is because the tension of the balloon is changed via the top of the main tube. The greater the tension, the higher the tone and the more you have to blow into the saxophone to make it sound.

12. Now you can cut the finger holes. Building a pentatonic saxophone without any other tools is almost impossible and not the goal of this outdoor project. My saxophones are never tuned and still sound amazingly beautiful when you play them.

Cut three to five holes in the main tube. The first hole should be about 1½" (4cm) from the lower end of the tube, and the remaining holes should be ¾"–1" (2–2.5cm) apart. First, draw the outlines of the finger holes. They should be exactly opposite the mouthpiece. Then use the fine-cutting technique to whittle a finger recess at the desired point.

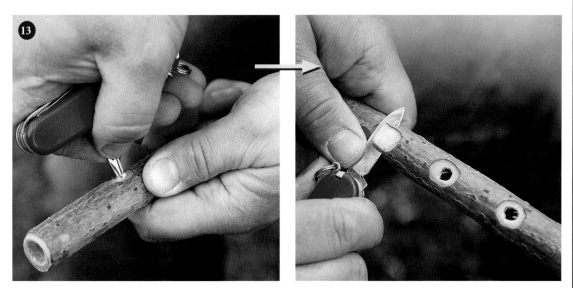

13. Now make a hole with the awl. The finger holes need to be a certain size so that the sound can change when the hole is open. The holes should be at least ³⁄₁₆" (5mm) in diameter. Making holes in the main tube will create excess protruding fibers.

15. Now you can earn a few pennies as a street musician. Maybe people will just pay you to stop bothering them with your free jazz experiments. Have fun with your saxophone!

14. Remove these as best you can with the sharp back of the saw, a stick, or another tool.

WILLOW FLUTE

I have heard from many older people in my workshops about making special flutes in their childhood with their father or another caregiver. When I asked for more detail, it usually turns out that they were building willow flutes. The best time to build a willow flute is in spring, when the willows are in full force and the first leaves begin to sprout. The core is easiest to remove at this time of year. This flute can also be made with ash or maple wood.

The length and diameter of the flute are not set in stone. The measurements in the following instructions only give an indication of the possible dimensions.

What You Need

All you need to make a willow flute is a straight willow branch without side branches and a Swiss Army Knife. The branch for my willow flute is about as thick as my thumb.

I. Whittle a beak-shaped mouthpiece at the end of the branch so you don't have to put the whole branch into your mouth when playing the flute.

2. Shorten the branch to about 8" (20cm). Make a cut all the way around the bark about 4¾" (12cm) from the mouthpiece. Put enough pressure on the blade so that the incision goes all the way to the wood.

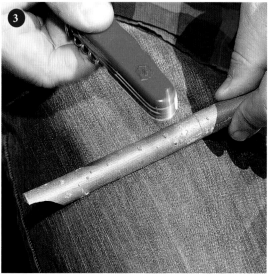

3. Now carefully tap on the bark between the cut and the mouthpiece with the flat part of the Swiss Army Knife. This tapping will make the bark separate from the wood more easily. In the photo, I had tapped around the branch for about three minutes until the bark could be removed.

4. Grasp the branch below the incision with one hand and hold the part you were tapping with the other hand (tightly). Now try to loosen the upper part by twisting hard. If that doesn't work, keep tapping until the bark can be removed. The part you remove the bark sleeve from will be the slide.

5. Now whittle a notch that will produce the sound when the flute is finished. To do this, slip the bark sleeve back on and make a stop cut ¾"–1¼" (2–3cm) from the end of the mouthpiece. To do this, press the knife vertically into the wood.

6. Use the fine-cutting technique to make a diagonal cut up to the stop cut.

7. You can now remove the bark sleeve.

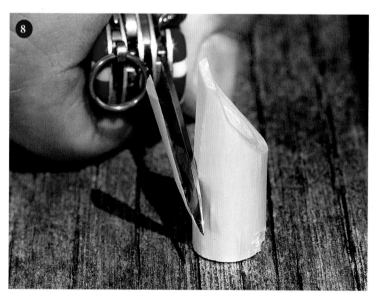

8. Saw through the wood where you made the cut. This will give you the so-called "block." Carefully split off a segment of the block about ¹⁄₁₆" (2mm) deep for the air vent.

9. If the gap pulls outward when splitting off, whittle out the gap surface a little more.

10. Now you should slightly tilt the sharp saw edge on the slide and carefully reinsert the block back into the bark sleeve. This photo shows a cross section of a willow flute.

Now if you blow into the mouthpiece, you can change the pitch by moving the slide up and down. This is not an instrument that will work forever. Once the wood and bark dry, the slide can no longer be moved up and down. Usually, willow flutes work for a day, after which you have to whittle a new flute. Now that you know how to whittle this classic instrument, it'll be no problem for you to whittle a new flute the next day.

BIRD WHISTLE

The bird whistle is a small flute, the end of which is submerged in water. The air blown in through the air duct causes the water to bubble and changes the pitch of the pipe so that it sounds similar to the chirping of a skylark. Most of these bird water pipes are made of clay or plastic. It was my goal to create such a flute using only common materials found in nature.

What You Need

For this project, an empty snail shell will serve as the water tank. For the flute, you need a thin hazel wood branch with a diameter of about $\frac{5}{32}$"–$\frac{1}{4}$" (4–6mm), a branch with a slightly thinner diameter for the block, and a piece of the soft, felt-like material of a tree mushroom. Naturally, the only tool you need is a Swiss Army Knife.

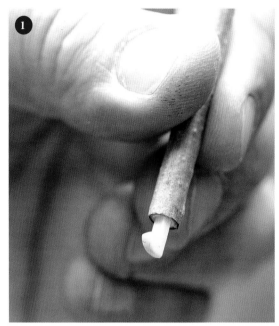

1. Start with the small flute. Cut an approximately 2½" (6cm) long piece from the hazel branch. Remove the soft core. Because of its small diameter, you need to use a toothpick, tweezers, and ballpoint pen insert for this. First, drill and push with the toothpick from both sides. Then, try to push the pen through the hole.

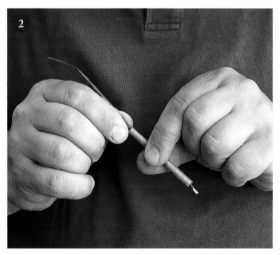

2. Scrape the rest of the core away with a small stick.

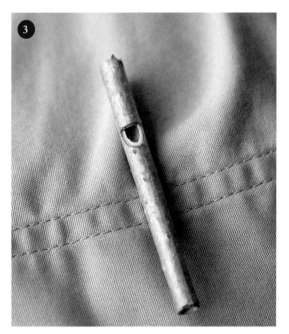

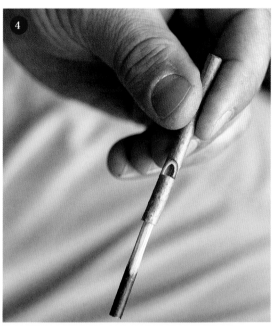

3. With the stop cut and fine cut, make a small notch about ⅝" (1.5cm) from the end of the tube.

4. Whittle the block that will later be pushed into the mouthpiece up to the notch. On one side, the block goes up to the stop cut of the notch. On the other side, the block sticks out of the main pipe about ⅜"–¾" (1–2cm). The diameter of the block must be as accurate as possible. The pipe must not tear when the block is pressed in, and it must also make an airtight seal with the block. Carve an air hole on the block before inserting it.

5. Now push the block into the mouthpiece. The block should be pushed right up to the notch. If you now hold the flute closed and blow at the top, you should hear a faint whistle. Don't worry, the sound will be much louder with the snail shell.

6. Cut off a ¼"–⁵⁄₁₆" (6–8mm) thick piece of mushroom. For this pipe, I'm not using tinder fungus, but red band fungus, which is more commonly found in Switzerland. Try to cut a closure for the snail shell hole that's as exact as possible. (Note: Only use a mushroom you know is safe.)

7. Try to imprint the exact shape of the shell onto the mushroom. Then, eyeball the proper size.

8. Once the mushroom stopper fits, very carefully make a hole through the center of the mushroom with the awl.

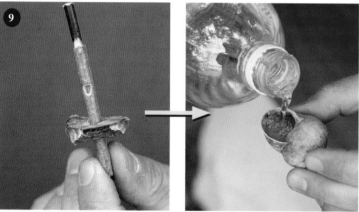

10. Then, press the stopper back into the hole, so that the water won't jump out of the shell when playing.

9. Press the flute through the hole and fill the shell with water.

11. Now you can play your bird whistle. If you're not happy with the sound, experiment with the block (position and size of the air vent) as well as the notch on the flute (bigger or smaller). The flute I made for these instructions sounded like a whole nest of hungry baby birds. PS: No other bird sings as much while flying as the skylark. I hope you have the stamina of a skylark when practicing with this bird whistle!

KAZOO

At a medieval festival, I whittled reed flutes with the visitors. An older man came to my booth and tried to explain in broken German that he also used to make an instrument out of reeds. He tried to explain it to me with a reed, but he couldn't make himself clear. Because I was whittling with other people and didn't have much time, the man eventually disappeared into the crowd. I was pretty sure he wanted to explain to me how he used to build kazoos out of reeds.

Later I tried to whittle such a kazoo. It took me a couple of tries before I could whittle a window into the wooden part of the reed without damaging the paper layer inside. I was surprised by how good my first reed kazoo sounded! During my research on the Internet, I discovered another method of improvising a kazoo with a bag. I would now like to show you both methods.

Reed Kazoo

What You Need

To make a reed kazoo, you need a dry reed and a Swiss Army Knife. Reeds grow like bamboo, with segments known as internodes. These segments are separated by nodes. For a kazoo, you need the section between two nodes.

1. You cannot saw reeds. The best way to cut the reeds is to cut the stalk diagonally with a sharp Swiss Army Knife. Once you have cut the nodes, you should be able to blow through the pipe. The actual length of the tube doesn't matter. I have made kazoos that were only about 3¼" (8cm) long.

2. Take off the easily removable outer skin. Because the reeds can be very sharp after you cut them, I recommend burning the tip with a lighter.

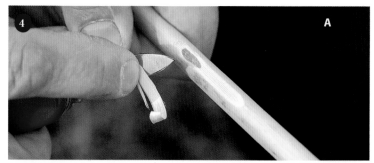

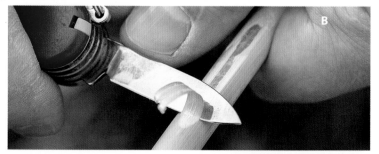

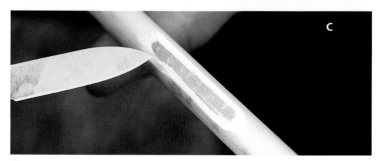

3. On the inside of the reed, there is a waterproof wax skin that seals the cell wall from the inner cavity. You want to try and create a "window" in the reed without damaging this skin. Be patient! It usually takes me several tries before I get it right. But where one reed grows, there are usually thousands of others. So, if you need to start over, you shouldn't have trouble finding another reed to work on. Use the whittling technique that you are most comfortable with. I like to whittle against body during this step (see page 194), but you need a lot of practice for this carving technique.

4. If you need to enlarge a window that's too small (A), I use the fine-cutting technique (B) to whittle until the window is the desired size (C). Usually, the window is about ⁵⁄₃₂"–³⁄₁₆" (4–5mm) wide and ¾"–1" (2–2.5cm) long. You'll know how big the window needs to be by playing the kazoo: just hum into it.

How to Kazoo

You don't blow into a kazoo—you hum into it. With the vibration of your voice, the "window," a small layer of skin, begins to vibrate as well. This membrane does not produce its own sound, but it amplifies and changes the tone of your voice. The result is a funny, distorted sound. The pitch depends entirely on the tone you sing into it. "Toot" powerfully and without restraint into your kazoo and you will quickly notice if your voice becomes distorted or not.

Elder Wood Kazoo

What You Need

To make an elder wood kazoo, you need a thinly walled elder wood tube, a piece of string, a Swiss Army Knife, and a piece of suitable material (like a plastic bag) for the membrane. In this tutorial, I will use a piece of plastic from a dog waste bag. Without getting too scientific, I would argue that any material that is very thin and makes a crackling sound when crumpled up would make a suitable membrane for your kazoo (parchment paper or thin, all-purpose plastic bags).

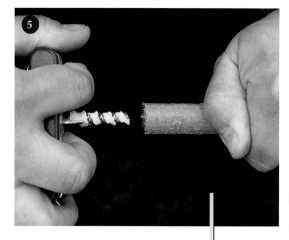

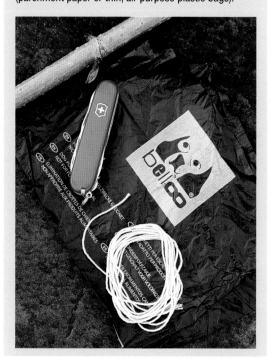

5. Let's start with the pipe. Cut a piece of elder wood about 6"–8" (15–20cm) long. Now remove the wood core. You can easily remove the first 1½" (4cm) on each side with the corkscrew. Then turn the saw into the hole as far as it will go on both sides. Finally, take a thin branch and simply push out the rest of the core. Clean the inside of the tube as well as possible.

6. Now cut a window into the pipe. In my experience, where you put the window in the pipe doesn't matter. Saw two boundary cuts with the saw that are about 1¼" (3cm) apart.

7. Use the fine-cutting technique to cut out the window.

8. Now cut a big enough piece of membrane, about 2" (5cm) wide, with the scissors—in this example, using the plastic dog waste bag.

9. Place the membrane over the window, wrap it twice around the branch, and fasten it with string, glue, or adhesive tape.

10. The tighter the membrane is, the higher the pitch of your kazoo.

11. Now vigorously hum "hmmm hmm, hmmmm" into the kazoo. This is how you can test if your kazoo is working or not. If the kazoo doesn't make any noise, it could be that the membrane isn't airtight enough. Have fun with your kazoo!

ELDER WOOD FLUTE

Elder wood flutes that produce only one tone are easy to make. Making an elder wood flute in the style of a recorder that can produce multiple tones is much more complicated.

I consulted a professional flute maker for this project and after many failed attempts, actually decided to remove it from this book. I couldn't figure out the reason why it wasn't working. It was extremely difficult to make the notch that creates sound in a finished flute with only a Swiss Army Knife. Later I tried again. I had an idea how I could make the notch differently. The flute I then made had by far the best sound of any before it. After a few more attempts, I was convinced that with this method, any skilled whittler could make a recorder out of an elder wood branch, so I decided to put the project back in the book.

What You Need

To build an elder wood flute, you need an elder branch for the pipe, a thinner hazel branch for the block, and some string for the air hole. For the pipe, I prefer to use a straight young elderberry branch with a diameter of about ¾" (2cm). Young branches often have a lot of pith and just a thin 1/16"–5/32" (2–4mm) layer of wood. This material is ideal for building a flute.

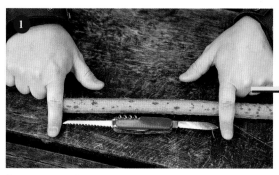

1. Saw off a 9" (23cm) long piece of elder wood for the tube and remove the core. Use the corkscrew for the first 1½" (4cm) on both sides of the branch. Twist it in on each side and pull it out multiple times. Then use the saw to remove more of the core. Now you have removed 2¾" (7cm) of core on both sides. Theoretically, there is still 3½" (9cm) of core left in the middle of the pipe that you still need to remove.

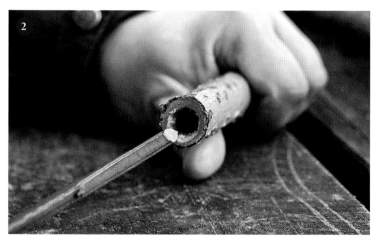

2. Because I don't want to use any tools other than the Swiss Army Knife for these projects, I remove the rest of the core with a sharply whittled dry hardwood branch. You can also use a thick wire, a long screw, or a drill.

3. Once you've created an open tube, scrape off the remaining core on the walls of the pipe with a branch and blow out any excess material. The pipe needs to be as clean as possible for the flute to work properly!

4. About 1½" (4cm) from the upper end, make a small hole with the awl.

5. Place the small blade on one side of this hole and split the pipe wall up to the end of the pipe. Do the same on the other side of the hole.

6. Remove the wall between the cuts.

7. Now widen the gap with the small blade until it is about as wide as the can opener on the Victorinox Swiss Army Knife.

8. Whittle out the corners as precisely as possible. This will later become the edge of the notch.

9. The ⁵⁄₃₂" (4mm) wood chisel found in some Victorinox models would be suitable for carving the notch. However, for this project, I will assume that you do not have a wood chisel in your Swiss Army Knife. Therefore, cut into the branch to the left and right of the gap with the blade so that you can whittle the sloping surface of the notch.

10. Find the section of the hazel branch that fits perfectly into this hole. This branch will become the so-called "block" for the mouthpiece.

11. Push the branch up to ⁵⁄₃₂"–³⁄₁₆" (4–5mm) before the notch's edge.

12. Saw it so it sticks out by ¾" (2cm). Whittle the sides of the gap flat.

13. You should be able to see a small space between the notch's edge and the block.

14. Now split off the top third of the piece of hazel wood. This is the airflow cover.

15. The length of the cover should be exactly as long as the depth of the block.

16. Attach the cover with tightly wound string over the air hole.

17. Now, make the tone holes with the awl. The holes must be a certain size so that the airflow at the hole breaks off cleanly and a clear tone is produced. Be careful when making the holes and don't use too much pressure because they can tear easily. Placing the holes in such a way that you wind up with a perfectly tuned flute is almost impossible with a Swiss Army Knife alone. I place the first hole about 1¼" (3cm) from the end of the flute. Then, I mark three additional holes ¾" (2cm) apart.

18. Use the fine-cutting technique to whittle a finger recess.

19. Try to remove the fibers that protrude inwards as best as possible with the blade or the saw.

20. Now your flute is finished. You should be very proud of yourself if your flute is playable. If your elder wood flute does not work properly, don't get discouraged and be sure to try again right away. Building a playable recorder-style elder wood flute with a Swiss Army Knife is, in my opinion, one of the most difficult whittling projects there is!

DANDELION TRUMPET

As kids, we often annoyed our parents with our dandelion trumpet concerts. With the stem of a dandelion, you can only make one shrill sound. When multiple kids are playing this instrument, it can be very annoying.

I wanted to see if a trumpet could be made based on the principle of the dandelion stem, but create multiple sounds. It was easy: producing different tones with the dandelion trumpet was relatively simple to achieve. The problem, however, was that the pointed ends of the stems tore and curled up after a short time. With a simple trick I found a solution to this problem. Voilà, here is the guide to this fun five-minute project.

It doesn't make sense to name specific dimensions for diameter, length, or hole spacing. Every trumpet sounds a little different. In my experiments, relatively short trumpets (I'm talking about 4"–6" [10–15cm]) had a richer, stronger tone than long trumpets. The shorter the trumpet, the higher the pitch. Dandelion plants that still had yellow flowers had slightly fresher, crisper stems than withered dandelion plants. I achieved better results with the harder stems than with soft stems.

What You Need

For this project, you need a strong dandelion stem and a Swiss Army Knife.

1. Use the scissors or the knife to cut the stem below the flower.

2. Remove a ⅜"–¾" (1–2cm) long tube from the thick part of the stem and place it over the thin part.

3. Now cut the stem ³⁄₁₆"–⁵⁄₁₆" (5–8mm) above this covered part.

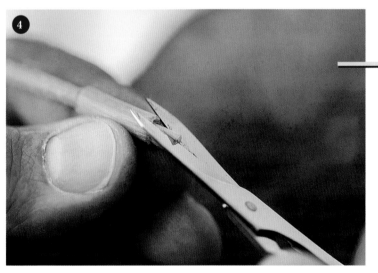

4. Take the scissors, press down the end of the stem with your fingers, and cut a symmetrical point. You can also do this with the knife.

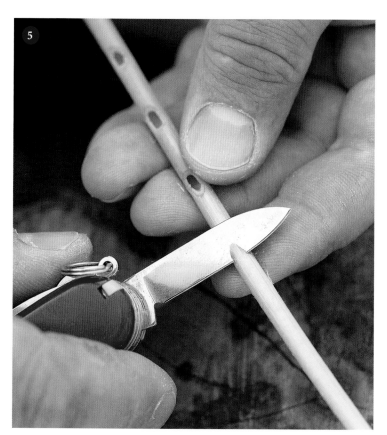

5. Put the mouthpiece in your mouth, lightly press the stem together with your lips, and try to blow as hard as you can to see if you can make a sound. If not, you can soften the tips of the mouthpiece by bending them back and forth. Once you've succeeded in producing a sound, begin to cut the holes in the stem. Make sure that you cut the holes very flat. Otherwise, the stem will be too weak for the flute to work properly. Make a cut from one side to the middle of the hole and repeat from the other side for the other half.

6. The dandelion trumpet functions as a double reed instrument. Clarinets, oboes, and bassoons also work this way. Two reeds made of flexible material vibrate due to a stream of air. The same goes for your instrument made from a dandelion stem. Thanks to the springiness of fresh stems, the tips are constantly pushed apart. This creates the column of air that produces sound. "Dandelion trumpet" is actually a misnomer: This instrument is more of a dandelion bassoon or a dandelion oboe. But because the sound is still more reminiscent of a trumpet, I'll leave the name as it is and wish you lots of fun playing it.

PROJECT: Dandelion Trumpet

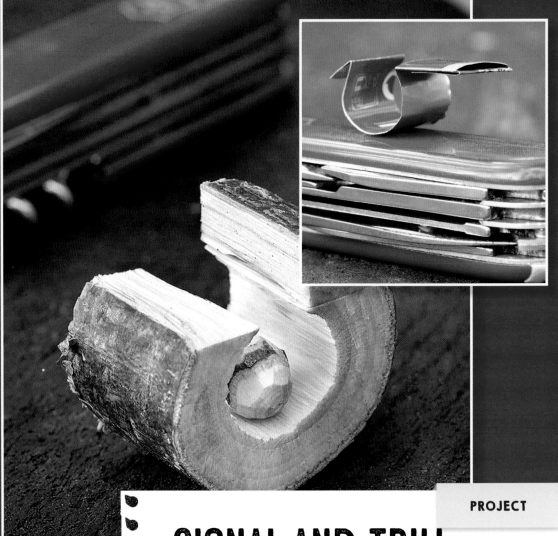

SIGNAL AND TRILL WHISTLES

A few years ago, I discovered instructions for building a signal whistle out of an aluminum can. I immediately made one for myself. The whistle worked great: if I blew really hard, the sound was deafening! So of course, I had the idea to create a version you could whittle from wood. My first attempts were successful, and I had so much fun creating this project that I would like to share it with you in this book.

Signal Whistle

What You Need

For the signal whistle, you need a piece of branch with a diameter of 1¼" –1½" (3–4cm) and a Swiss Army Knife. This project is easier if the branch is reasonably round and the pith is in the middle.

1. First cut off a ¾" (2cm) thick piece of the branch. Then, make a hole through the core with the awl. You can further enlarge the hole with the cutting edge of the awl. To widen the hole even more, carefully turn the saw inside the existing hole.

2. Whittle the hole even bigger with the small blade. It should have a diameter of at least ¹⁵⁄₃₂" (12mm). Don't make it too big—you want to be able to comfortably cover the hole with your index finger and thumb.

3. Now split off a piece to break the circle.

4. The gap created should not be wider than ¼" (6mm).

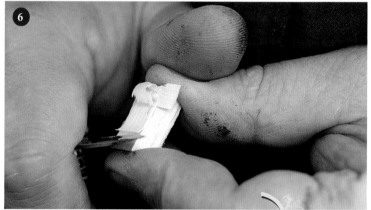

6. Use the fine-cutting technique against your thumb (see page 194) to cut an air hole in the small piece you split off.

5. Now you have to decide which side of the gap you want the airflow to be on. The wedge on the opposite side is the notch, the important part of the whistle that manipulates the air. The swirling of the air causes vibrations that create sound. In my experience, having a large air hole has never been a disadvantage. Place both pieces back together and split the side where the air hole should be right where the circle is broken.

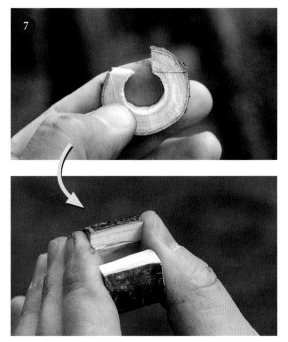

7. Place the air hole cover at the right spot and place your index finger and thumb over the hole. The cover should also be held in place between your fingers.

8. Blow into the air hole. If you don't hear a whistle, it might be that your fingers aren't making the whistle airtight or that all the air is flowing over the notch. Try to whittle the bottom of the air hole flat so that the flow of air can be broken by the notch and a small amount of air makes its way into the hole. Now your signal whistle should work properly. Try again if it's still not working.

Trill Whistle

With a small modification, you can turn your signal whistle into a trill whistle.

9. Whittle a small wooden ball that's bigger than the gap in the circle and place the ball in the hole. Now if you blow hard into the whistle, the ball will make a trill sound. Whether a signal whistle or a trill whistle, all that matters is that it's loud!

PROJECT

RATTLE

For a special rotisserie grill, I wanted to make a freewheel, that is, a coupling that only works in one direction. When I was finished, I noticed that the tool sounded like a rattle when spun in the air, so I modified the design slightly and developed a great new project. Have fun making your own version!

What You Need

The rattle consists of four individual parts: gear, axle, tongue, and body. You need three sticks to build the rattle depicted here: a 1½" (4cm) thick stick for the gear wheel and the body, a ¾" (2cm) thick stick for the tongue, and a ⅜" (1cm) thick stick for the axle. Additionally, you need some string and a Victorinox Swiss Army Knife.

The key component of the rattle is the gear. Use a branch as dry as possible for this. The gear will also work with fresh wood but, in my experience, it almost always splits when it dries and the wood contracts.

1. Saw off a ½" (1.5cm) thick disc with a diameter of about 1½" (4cm) from the thicker branch.

2. Use an improvised compass to draw the outer diameter of the gear. You can make the compass with a wood chip, the Swiss Army Knife pin, and the Swiss Army Knife pen.

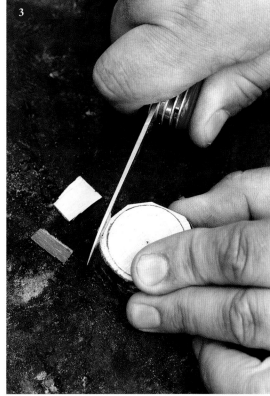

3. Split the outer material along the marked circle. Either use a stick as a hammer to insert the knife blade into the wood or, if you're strong enough, press the blade into the wood by hand.

4. Divide the outer circle as accurately as possible into eight segments.

5. Make another circle between the height of the gear teeth and the outer diameter.

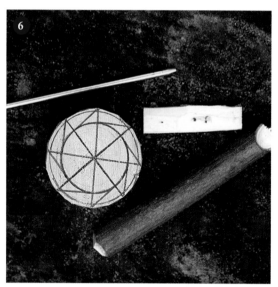

6. Draw the gear teeth.

7. The vertical lines from the outer rim to the inner circle are sawed first. Then, split the wood along the diagonal lines. I have also tried to make rattles with symmetrical teeth that work in both directions. The problem with this design is that the gear wheel can tear when splitting off the teeth, so I decided to use asymmetrical teeth for this project.

8. Now make a hole in the middle of the gear wheel. This will later be used for the axle.

9. To stop the axle from spinning inside the gear, make this hole oval. To whittle an oval hole, first make a round hole and cut or scrape away wood with the awl. The diameter on the wide side of the oval should be about ⅜" (1cm). The diameter of the axle must therefore also be ⅜" (1cm).

10. Now take the stick for the axle and whittle it into a matching oval shape.

11. I usually make the body of the rattle of the same branch as the gear wheel. Cut an approximately 6" (15cm) long, straight piece of the branch for the body. Making the groove for the gear wheel is easier if you split the wood in the middle (see also "splitting with homemade wooden wedges," page 191).

12. Saw both halves through the middle.

13. Split off the inner part from each half.

14. If you put both halves back together, you will get the desired groove. I cannot give exact dimensions. The size of the groove varies depending on the size and thickness of the gear.

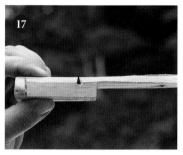

17. To prevent the tongue from moving from side to side, saw a dovetail groove on either side of the outer surface. You can do this by tilting the saw blade from side to side while sawing.

15. Now whittle a surface for the tongue on the top of the rattle halves. To do this, hold the two halves together and cut a small groove with the saw ³⁄₁₆" (5mm) from the front. This creates a stop so that the tongue cannot slide backward.

16. Use the large knife to split off the area up until the groove for the tongue. Whittle a bit more to adjust the area as needed.

18. Now look for a suitable branch and press a piece of it into the holes on either side.

19. Use the awl to drill a hole for the axle on both parts.

20. I used the saw to enlarge this pilot hole to about ⅜" (10mm). Continue to check the position of the two holes by holding the two rattle body halves together and pushing a branch through.

21. Insert the axle with the gear.

22. To make the tongue, use a straight, finger-thick branch. The length of the branch should be the distance between the rear stop and the center of the gear. Split the branch lengthwise. Whittle the surface of the split area flat so that you can no longer see any of the wood core. You can also whittle the round side flat so that you're left with a ⅛" (3mm) thick board.

23. Now you can put all the parts together. Secure the tongue with string and see if your rattle works. Have fun with your homemade rattling machine!

ACORN WHISTLE

I remember a trick I learned in Boy Scouts: you can make a really loud sound with the top of an acorn and both thumbs. You can also put the top of the acorn in your fist and blow into your fist between two fingers. This is also super loud. One of my workshop participants showed me that the principle of the acorn whistle also works with a whittled hollow body.

What You Need

All you need is a ½"–¾" (1.5–2cm) thick branch and a Swiss Army Knife.

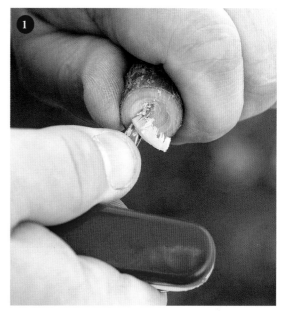

1. Cut off a piece of the branch about 1¼" (3cm) long. One side should be cut as straight as possible. Then use the awl to make an outward-facing, cone-shaped indentation in the wood so that only a very thin edge is left.

2. Whittle it smooth with the small blade because its small size allows you to cut more precisely. The fine-cutting technique against your thumb (page 194) is a good choice for this step.

3. Now you can start testing your whistle. Hold the piece of branch between your index finger and thumb with the whittled indentation facing you. Press the two backs of your thumbs together and form a "V" with the top of your thumbs. The lower point of the "V" should lie above the center of the indentation. Your thumbs, along with the whittled indentation, form a cavity with a small V-shaped opening.

 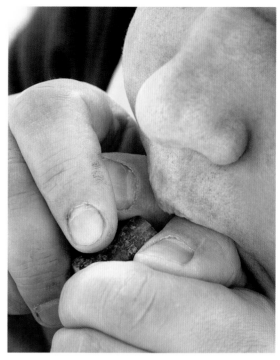

4. Press your lower lip against the knuckles of your thumbs, take a deep breath, place the upper lip on the part of your thumbs angled outward, and blow vigorously and directly into the triangular opening. The airflow swirls around in the cavity and produces the whistling sound.

Finding Your Tune

If you can't produce a whistle, find an acorn top. If you can't get any sound from there either, it's because of your whistling technique. If you succeed with an acorn top, it is not because of your whistling technique, but because of your hole in the branch. If this is the case, readjust the hole. You may have to tinker with it a bit.

The larger the cavity, the deeper the pitch of the whistle. Such a whistle can be very useful if you want to draw attention to yourself or if you want to keep a wild animal at a distance. I tried the latter with my neighbor's cat. The whistle has an impressive effect on both people and animals.

KNOTWEED WHISTLE

I was looking for a plant that was not poisonous and would be good for this project: easy to tune, with a hollow stem. Pretty quickly I found the Japanese knotweed aka "knotweed." Because Japanese knotweed doesn't usually have an airtight chamber between its internodes, you need to close off the end with your finger, unlike if you were working with chervil, so that the air doesn't escape.

I only recently discovered this kind of whistle. A participant in my class told me that he whittled this kind of whistle as a child. Urs Weber, a good friend of mine who helped me develop some of the projects in this book, knew about the chervil whistle and was able to give me a few tips. Thanks, Urs!

I am fascinated by the simplicity of this "30-second project" and also by the powerful sound of this whistle.

What You Need

All you need for the knotweed pipe is a sturdy Japanese knotweed stem and a Swiss Army Knife.

The stem in the photo is rather small. This photo was taken in the summer, and the plants had not grown very much. In autumn they are a lot bigger.

1. Find a strong, undamaged hollow section of the stem.

2. Make sure that you cut it off above the growth node on one side and below the growth node on the other. The open end will become the mouthpiece, and the growth node at the end will close off the airflow. If the growth node doesn't form an airtight blockage, you need to hold your finger against the hole.

3. Now carefully cut the stem lengthwise. The Swiss Army Knife blade should only penetrate through the outer wall and not cut through the entire stem.

4. First, cut the stem about 2" (5cm) long. Be aware that the slit should be in the middle of the stem.

5. Blow hard into the tube. If you don't hear a sound, blow harder. If you still don't hear a sound, try turning the tube and blowing from the other side. If you're still not successful, carefully lengthen the cut and try the whistle again. Continue to do this if it still doesn't work. Sometime you need a little patience before you can get the stem to whistle. Depending on the size of the tube, the slit can be up to 4" (10cm) long.

The pitch depends on the diameter and length of the tube as well as the length of the slit. The knotweed whistle only works if the stem is still juicy and crisp. I think it's cool when you have a trick for bringing sound out of a plant.

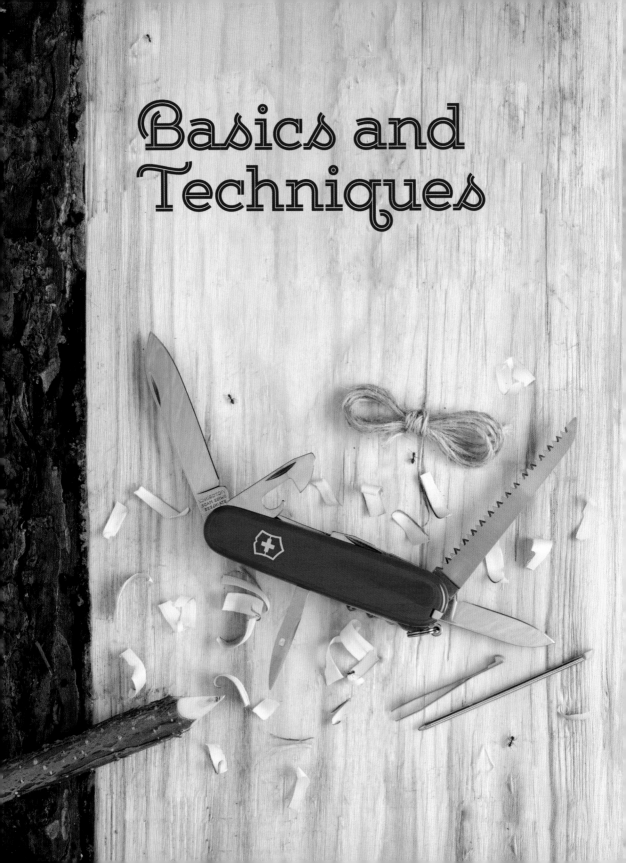

Basics and Techniques

These are the kinds of things parents and other adults say when kids are using a Swiss Army Knife. Anyone attempting to whittle for the first time will probably still manage to cut themselves despite all the safety rules and precautions in the world. This can hardly be avoided. However, learning to whittle and use a Swiss Army Knife should not be accompanied by discomfort, fear, or uncertainty. An anxious attitude has a negative impact on learning and gives neither the child nor the adult the necessary peace and calmness needed to work safely. Children learn especially by mimicking the behavior of adults. The same is true for learning to use Swiss Army Knives. Children learn anxious, haphazard styles of working as easily as they learn calm, safe techniques.

Adults who have little to no experience with the knives can only be a role model to a limited extent. To the parents who own a Swiss Army Knife and only use it to cut or skewer sausage: I would like to ask that you go through this book and practice the techniques for yourself first. When your children see how skillfully you handle the knife, they will also want to learn to use the knife properly.

It is important to first discuss safety rules with the child and to hand over a part of the responsibility when handing over the knife. It should be a positive learning atmosphere. And soon you will be surprised by the progress your child is making.

Safety Rules for Whittling

There are clear rules for whittling with children. It can be beneficial for an adult to develop the rules together with a child and not just simply present them with a list of hard and fast rules. Children often know two or three of the rules already and can be part of the conversation, making them more aware the rules. It's easier for children to follow rules that they helped develop because their own beliefs and ideas are incorporated. Of course, the wording doesn't have to exactly match these predetermined rules. To further help kids enjoy developing the rules, I created a comic with some friends called *The Whittle Kids*. In it, we illustrate child-friendly rules with a funny short story. On the website *www.feliximmler.ch* you can download the comic for free and print it as often as you like. In order to understand the reasoning behind the individual rules, each of the nine points has an explanation.

"Watch your fingers!"

"That's dangerous, let me do it!"

"Give me the knife, you're not strong enough!"

"Watch out, this is how you fold the awl!"

▶ YouTube www.youtube.com/feliximmler
🏠 www.feliximmler.ch

I always whittle with a sharp blade.

Sharp knives can be moved more precisely, they grip better, and you can work with less effort. Blunt knives pose a great danger because you need to apply more force and the knife slips more easily. To keep the blade sharp, don't use it to cut stone, metal, or glass because this will make the blade dull very quickly. Never stick the blade of your Swiss Army Knife into the ground: this will make it dull.

If you whittle, you sit.

Whittling requires undivided attention. When you stand up, fold the knife away. If you slip or stumble, you won't have control of the blade anymore and could give yourself some series cut or stab injuries.

Keep enough distance from other people.

To check whether you have enough distance to the next person, extend your whittling arm and draw a semicircle in the air in front of you. If you don't touch anyone, you have enough space. For larger groups of children, it is recommended that a small, protected work area be set up for the whittlers. Those who are not whittling should be careful not to cross the line.

When whittling, I always point the knife away from my body and from my hand that's holding the wood.

Never cut in the direction of your hand or body unless you're very skilled with the knife.

Only unfold one tool at a time.

Always fold away any knives you're not using. You could injure yourself with the other tools.

I always put my knife away when I don't need it.

Leaving a sharp knife blade lying around is dangerous because you could hurt yourself or others.

I always hand someone my Swiss Army Knife with the blade folded away.

There are techniques for handing someone a regular knife safely. Swiss Army knives, however, should only be handed over when they're closed.

I don't scratch or saw into trees or other plants.

The bark on a tree is not there so that you can draw a heart or write your name on it. Tree bark is similar to our human skin and is the tree's protection. The nutrients for the tree are also transported through a layer underneath the bark.

The knife is a tool, not a weapon.

Don't threaten or hurt any person or animal with the Swiss Army Knife. The Swiss Army Knife is also not a throwing knife.

You should whittle in front of you with your legs spread.

The Correct Posture for Whittling

"If you're whittling, you're sitting!" To be a good role model, as well as for their own safety, even adults should practice sitting when they whittle, so find a sturdy seat. The seat shouldn't be too high for children: they should be able to rest their feet on the floor shoulder-width apart. A seat height of about 8"–12" (20–30cm) is perfect for children.

Keep the object you want to whittle as short as possible and support the forearm of your resting hand with your knee. This gives you more stability for the object you are whittling. The hand that is holding the wood should always be behind the knife—never in front of it. You should whittle toward the ground. There should be nothing in the knife's path. Never whittle against your thighs in your lap. Arteries that transport a lot of blood run through the inner thigh. Whittle in front of your knees!

It's best to use some sort of pad to kneel on instead of kneeling on dirty or wet ground. Also, in this position, make sure not to whittle against your thighs and keep enough distance from the person or object closest to you.

You can also whittle off to the side of your legs. Working at your side requires that there is enough space between you and the next person.

If you have no place to sit, you can also whittle when kneeling.

Opening and Closing the Tools

There are many ways to open and close a Swiss Army Knife blade. An experienced Swiss Army Knife user does this automatically without having to look or think about the movements. In general, it's important that the Swiss Army Knife's body is firmly in your hand when opening or closing the knife. Children with little experience whittling should always be supervised when opening or closing a Swiss Army Knife. For this reason, it is recommended to teach children from the very beginning to use the following opening and closing methods.

Opening the Tools

1. The hand that holds the knife should hold it between four fingertips on one side and the palm of the hand and the thumb on the other side. This should be done with the knife facing away from the body.

2. To unfold the blade, place the thumbnail of your opposite hand into the recess and hold the blade tightly on the other side with your index finger.

3. Now you can pull out the blade in a semicircle movement.

4. The knife is fully opened when the blade makes a "click" that you can hear and feel.

This method applies to all tools that have a nail recess. With the saw, the round tip protrudes slightly so that it can be opened with your thumbnail.

Closing the Tools

Folding the tools closed is especially dangerous for children with little whittling experience. For this process, the child must always be able to see where the sharp edges are. Children must be able to check that their finger or any part of their hand is not in the way.

1. The Swiss Army Knife should be held the same way it is when unfolding a tool. Holding the knife this way gives you the best view of the knife shaft.

2. With the other hand, hold the back of the blade at the nail recess between your thumb and index finger.

3. Move the blade in a semicircle back into its housing. By holding the back of the knife until it is fully closed, the child has the movement under control and can always see where the tip is.

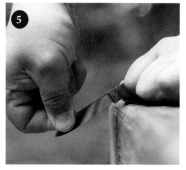

4. For children who don't yet have strong hands, it is not uncommon for the Swiss Army Knife to come out of their grip when closing the blade. For these children, I recommend the following technique: look for a raised area with a flat surface like a tree trunk, a table, a bench, or a flat rock. Place the body of the Swiss Army Knife on the surface so that the blade sticks out over the edge and the blade is pointing down. Hold the body of the Swiss Army Knife in place with one hand.

5. Use your other to hold the back of the blade at the nail recess between your thumb and index finger and press down on the blade until it reaches a 90° angle. Then, move the body of the Swiss Army Knife into your hand, continuing to hold the blade tightly between thumb and index finger, and finish folding the blade closed.

All tools should be easy to open and close as long as your Swiss Army Knife is clean and well oiled. If dried juice from cutting a fruit, resin, or other contaminants get into the folding mechanism of your Swiss Army Knife, it can make it impossible to open or close. Therefore, you should make sure to take care of your knife as described in the section "Cleaning Your Swiss Army Knife" on page 199.

The Hand Grip

In order to be able to properly transfer the force from your arm to the cutting edge of the knife, the knife must sit firmly in your hand. Many children I've worked with hold the knife too tentatively and hold it loosely in their hands. In order to be able to whittle effectively and safely, a firm but not too intense grip on the handle is necessary. You should also not hold the knife too far back on the handle, as this will reduce the cutting force.

The fist grip is the basic grip when working with Swiss Army Knife blades. To get a better feeling for the cutting motion and for better leverage, some people place their thumbs on the back of the knife. This technique is not wrong. You need to be aware that the blade might start to close if you put too much pressure on the back of the knife. When children are starting out, I prefer if they hold the Swiss Army Knife in their fists and do not place their thumb on the back of the blade. See what feels most comfortable to you.

 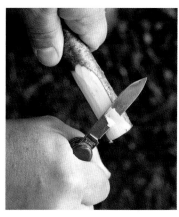

The knife is held correctly If only a small piece of the top of the handle can be seen in your closed grip.

Placing your thumb on the back of the knife isn't wrong, but beware of causing the knife to close.

The Most Important Swiss Army Knife Tools When Working with Wood

I will review the most important Swiss Army Knife tools and the associated techniques when working with wood. The rough cut, for example, does not necessarily need to be carried out with the large blade. You can also make a rough cut with the small blade. The same goes for the fine-cutting technique, which can be used with the large blade as well. But in general,

"rough cut with the large blade and fine cut with the small blade" is a good rule of thumb.

The large blade, small blade, wood saw, and awl are the indispensable tools for me when working with wood. I mainly used these four tools for the projects presented in this book. Additional functions such as the scissors, the pin, the ballpoint pen, or the tweezers are useful and helpful from time to time, but they are not essential to master the projects in this book.

Whittling Techniques with the Large Blade

The Rough Cut

The rough cut is a commonly used basic whittling technique that is good for beginners. The rough cut can be used to create a surface or a point. The knife blade is pressed forward with force and at the same time pulled sideways from the Ricasso (the non-sharpened part of the blade) to the tip of the knife until the knife emerges from the piece. I use the rough cut for rough shaping or if I want to remove a lot of material. The long cutting edge of the blade can produce large chips. A rough cut transfers maximum force to the cutting edge. It is not suitable for very fine cuts because the cutting motion can't be easily slowed or stopped.

The rough cut is only efficient if the cutting edge also moves longitudinally from the Ricasso to the tip of the blade during the forward movement (pulling cut; see tip on page 189).

The Technique

1. Hold the knife with the fist grip.

2. Place the blade flat on the surface of the wood and as close as possible to the handle.

3. During the forward motion, the blade is pulled through the wood in such a way that it moves from the handle to the tip throughout the movement. The wrist remains stiff.

4. The steeper the knife is set into the wood, the deeper the cut will go, which requires more effort.

The Power Cut

This is a very useful technique. I use it if I want to cut through a stick or if I want to remove a lot of material with short cuts. I hold the Swiss Army Knife so the cutting edge is facing the back of my hand holding it. The blade is slightly tilted down so it can penetrate the wood.

The Technique

1. Cross the blade and the wood in front of you. The knife should lie almost flat against the wood.

2. Now pull the wood and the knife away from each other at the same time.

3. Your forearms move outward across your chest and your shoulder blades contract.

4. With this technique, the point of contact with the blade also moves from the handle to the tip of the blade (pulling cut).

Pulling Cut

Have you ever tried to slice a loaf of bread by just pushing your knife through the middle of it? Probably not. If you have, then you'll have wound up with a piece of flattened bread. Most people intuitively move the knife back and forth when slicing a loaf. This results in a clean cut that doesn't squish the bread. This type of "pressing cut" where the blade is moved forward and backward is called a "pulling cut." This allows the blade to slice through the object more easily. This concept also applies to wood. This is most efficiently done when the sharp edge of the knife is utilized all the way from the Ricasso to the tip of the blade during the cutting movement.

This technique is perfectly safe when done properly because the knife blade points outward and you whittle away from your body. Because you are using the muscles in your back and shoulders to achieve this cut, there is a lot of force behind it.

Splitting (Batoning)

For many projects in this book, you need to split a branch to get the right materials. *Batoning* is the technical term in bushcraft for splitting wood with a knife. The knife is placed at the top of a branch or trunk and driven into the wood with a baton. To split wood this way, larger traditional full tang knives (when the metal of the blade extends into the handle) work much better than a Swiss Army Knife. The heavy forces that are placed on the knife are especially problematic for folding knives. With Victorinox Swiss Army Knives, you can easily split wood with a diameter of ¾" (2cm) with the large knife without causing any damage. Necessary caution and the right technique are required.

Technique of Splitting with the Unfolded Blade

1. Place the cut branch on a hard surface (e.g., a tree trunk). Place the blade directly into the core.

2. Then, carefully hit the back of the knife with a baton until the knife moves into the wood. The back of the knife must be hit directly to split the wood. You can help the process along by turning the knife slightly. But don't overdo it with too much force.

Splitting with Homemade Wooden Wedges

Some projects in this book require you to split a branch that is thicker than ¾" (2cm). Use whittled wooden wedges to do this. Your Swiss Army Knife will thank you! It is easier, more efficient, and better for your knife to whittle several small wedges than it is to make one large wedge. Simply saw a straight ¾"–1¼" (2–3cm) thick branch to the desired length and whittle a wedge shape into it on one side.

Technique of Splitting with Wooden Wedges

1. Fold out the Swiss Army Knife blade to only 90°. Place the blade into the core or the desired point in the wood.

2. Carefully hit the knife with a baton until it sinks into the wood. The back of the knife must be hit directly to split the wood. This way you avoid damaging the axle or the spring.

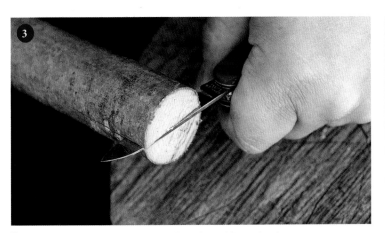

3. Then unfold the blade completely and carefully pull it out of the wood again.

4. Now drive the narrow wooden wedge into the gap. For pieces with large diameters, add one or two additional wedges.

Scraping

I prefer the large blade for scraping because the large blade doesn't slip as much.

1. Place the blade at a right angle on the surface of the wood.

2. Move the cutting edge back and forth across it with little pressure.

I use this technique when I need to smooth over a surface or remove bark from a branch. Because careful scraping only removes small chips, this technique is also suitable for fine projects like a bow. To prevent marks from appearing on the surface, the scraping direction must be changed multiple times. It's also a good idea to support the object you are scraping on a solid surface.

Whittling Techniques with the Small Blade

The small blade is often underestimated. Actually, it is the true carving blade on a Swiss Army Knife! But many people don't use it at all. The advantages of the small blade are evident in precise work. Because the Ricasso is narrower and the cutting edge shorter, the power transfer is more effective than with the large blade. The smaller-lever forces come into play, which push the wrist backward. For the same reason, the knife can be guided more precisely. The small blade is also not as long, which is why it is more agile in the wood. Curves are much easier to whittle with it than with the large blade. Because the small blade is much thinner, it also has less resistance when whittling. A shorter blade also means a reduced risk of accidents, since you need to be aware of a smaller cutting surface. Classic whittling knives with a fixed blade are also short for these reasons.

The Fine Cut

With fine cuts, the knife is held exactly the same as with rough cuts. The wrist of the hand holding the piece is supported on the knee.

1. Always whittle in front of your knees and never in your lap or on your thighs.

2. Hold the piece a few inches behind the whittling area when making a fine cut. The thumb of the hand holding the piece presses on the back of the blade.

The knife penetrates without moving sideways. This technique enables the blade to be guided safely and precisely, and the cut can be stopped precisely. The fine cut is suitable for making curves, grooves, or notches. In addition, fine cutting is the technique of choice when it comes to all types of bark patterns or when you want to write something in the wood.

Fine Cut against the Thumb

This technique is for experienced whittlers. For example, I use it to chamfer (bevel) a sharp edge on a stick. I carefully pull the cutting edge toward me with the force of the thumb of the carving hand. It is best if the thumb rests below the cutting point. This ensures that you do not cut yourself when finishing or if the knife slides.

Whittling against the Body

After everything that you now know about the basic techniques of whittling, it may seem absurd for you to learn about a carving technique "against the body." For experienced whittlers, this method has its uses. Decide for yourself to what extent it makes sense to familiarize your child with it.

I use this technique when the piece has too little space to hold onto during a fine cut. For example, I use it for fine-tuning the handle on a fork or spoon.

1. Support the piece against your chest. As a protection against cutting and to reduce the pressure of the piece against the chest, you can place leather or another material between your chest and the piece. Because the wrist is held rigid, the forearm stops the whittling movement in front of your chest every time the inside of the arm hits the chest.

2. This technique can be used to remove long, fine chips.

Techniques with the Saw Blade

The wood saws in Victorinox Swiss Army Knives are very sharp. For safety reasons, the saw should be folded away when not in use. You should try to only use it in a sawing motion. You shouldn't saw with too much pressure. Let the sharp saw blades do the work. Due to the coarse teeth, the saw is well suited for wet and fresh wood, but it also saws dry wood without any problems. The trapezoidal cross-section of the saw blade enables low-friction work without the saw blade jamming. These saws have a very long shelf life, which means that the saws stay sharp for a long time, provided that you really only saw wood with them. Injuries with the saw blade are often particularly painful and heal slowly because the many serrations on the saw do not simply cut the skin, but tear it open. It causes a "frayed" wound.

Stabilizing Your Tools

Tools for Securing a Workpiece
In order to prevent accidents when sawing with a Swiss Army Knife, the piece should be secured in place so that it does not move when sawing. The safest way to secure the piece is to clamp it in a vise or attach it to a stable base with a screw clamp. A sawhorse is also a safe option.

Securing a Workpiece without Technical Aids
The magic word for a successful saw cut is *stability*. You will be able to saw through a piece without the saw teeth getting stuck only if you keep the piece stable enough.

1. If possible, press the piece against a firm surface. This can be a large, flat stone, a small wall, a bench, a tree trunk, or a thick branch lying on the ground. If you hold the piece with one foot, you can use your body weight to put pressure on it and there is no danger of cutting yourself, unlike if you held it in your hand. Your shoe protects your foot. You also have both hands free.

2. Saw in the direction the wood is clamped in. In other words, saw vertically downward if you are pressing the stick down against a surface with your foot. In my opinion, securing the piece with your foot is the safest method of sawing without the use of technical aids.

Other Uses for the Saw Blade

I also use the saw as a kind of file or rasp for bushcraft. If I want to flatten a small area, I push the saw diagonally across the area, just like a file.

I sometimes use the saw blade as a drill or to widen a hole. I carefully turn the saw into the hole I previously started with the awl or into the core of an elder wood branch. You can use this method to make holes with a diameter of about ⅜" (1cm).

Sometimes I have to cut off a small stem or a sapling, maybe to make an arrow. I cannot press the branch against a surface, so I sort of saw in the air. Sawing off thin branches from a tree or shrub can be dangerous because the branch cannot be secured and moves around when sawing. Therefore, instead of sawing, it is advisable to cut off the branch with the large knife blade. In order to cut a branch up to approximately ¾" (2cm) in diameter with the knife blade, hold it under tension by bending it (A) and press the blade flat into the fiber on the tensioned side (B, C, D). Do not make the cut at a right angle through the wood like you would with the saw, but at only a slight angle. As a result, the fibers separate almost automatically.

Stabbing, Drilling, and Sewing with the Awl

The awl is very versatile. You can use it to drill, prick, scrape, clear blockages, clean, pre-drill, and even sew. I have used the awl on different materials, such as leather, cardboard, plastic, soapstone, aluminum, and of course for wood. The Victorinox awl has a cutting edge that cuts clockwise. It cuts into the material, so it works by slicing.

Warning: folding the awl closed can cause injury if you're not careful. That is why you have to support the awl when drilling by clamping it between your thumb and forefinger. The other three fingers are placed around the Swiss Army Knife body. When removing the point of the awl from an object, make sure that you don't prick yourself. Working with the awl, just like carving with the blades, requires maximum concentration.

Secure the awl by holding it between your thumb and forefinger.

You can turn the workpiece in the opposite direction to drill a hole.

A hole is drilled by applying some pressure in the direction of drilling and turning the hand or awl. If you hold the workpiece in your hand, you can also turn it in the opposite direction. Then, the pressure is released, the hand is turned back to the starting position, and this drilling movement is repeated until the hole is finished.

The Safety Technique

I recommend teaching children who have little whittling experience this safety technique. It has only one small difference from the previously explained technique: you hold the knife with the awl unfolded the other way around, so that the corkscrew and the sharp blade of the awl face upward. The awl is clamped between the thumb and forefinger as usual, and the remaining three fingers do not grip the longer part of the handle, but the short one, so that the corkscrew and the key ring are above the fist.

If the awl slips back in, it folds closed without any fingers in the way. Holding the awl this way has the ergonomic disadvantage when working because the cutting movement takes place counterclockwise at the top and not clockwise at the bottom toward you. For this reason, most people hold the awl the other way around. Experience has shown that children get used to this safer version fairly quickly.

Children should grip the shorter part of the handle when using the awl.

Sewing with the Awl

The awl has a hole. A string or thread can be passed through this, and two materials can be connected with a rough seam. Here is the technique for sewing with a Swiss Army Knife awl.

1. Hold the unfolded awl so that the nail recess is facing you, and thread the string through the hole from behind. The part of the thread that comes out of the hole at the front is the "end." The other part of the thread follows along with the awl, just like with a sewing machine.

2. Use the awl to puncture the materials that you want to sew together, and pull the end up so that it lies on top of the material. The end should be a little longer than the length of the finished seam.

3. The sewing direction is from right to left. To sew, pull the awl back completely, move it by ⅜" (1cm) and insert it again through the materials.

4. Now only pull the awl back to the eye of the needle. A small loop is created on the front and on the back.

5. Thread the end through the loop on the front of the awl.

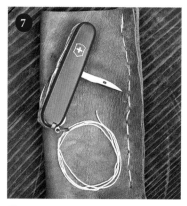

6. Pull the awl back completely, tighten the threads of the seam, move the awl ⅜" (1cm), and make the next stitch.

7. Continue this way until the desired seam length is achieved.

Caring for Your Swiss Army Knife

Cleaning Your Swiss Army Knife

Your Swiss Army Knife will do its job longer and better if you give it some basic care. Cleaning the knife is essential. For example, when cutting or peeling fruit, fruit juice can flow into the knife body, which sticks to the knife's tools after it dries. Resin-rich wood or sugary foods can also stick to the tools or make them dirty. To clean your Swiss Army Knife, place it in warm water with a little bit of liquid soap for a few hours and then open and close the tools several times. You will soon notice that the knife opens and closes again effortlessly. It is best to put a drop of oil on the sliding surfaces after cleaning and drying. Dirt in the knife shaft can best be removed with an old toothbrush under running water when the tools are unfolded. Do not put your knife in the dishwasher. The high temperatures and the aggressive detergents especially damage the handle scales; they will bend and become dull.

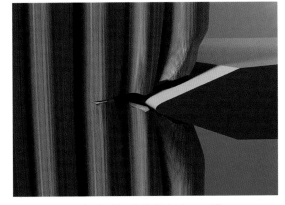

When carving wood with a blunt knife blade, the wood fibers are severely compressed and break before they are cut. The cut surface in the wood becomes rough. Working with a blunt blade requires a lot of effort, and the knife is difficult to guide.

Sharpening the Tools

Any tool you use for cutting will need to be sharpened eventually. In the following section, I will explain how to sharpen your Swiss Army Knife. Of course, the other tools like the awl, can opener, wood chisel, and scissors can also be sharpened if necessary. Sharpening any tool by hand requires a lot of practice and sharpening experience. Knife sharpening is a science in itself—entire books have been written about it. I will assume in this book that you have little or no knife-sharpening experience. That is why I will keep this chapter short, simple, and pragmatic. I will explain how to use a Victorinox quick sharpener, which anyone can use to sharpen a blunt knife and which I have been very satisfied with.

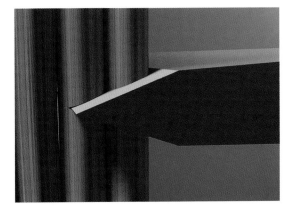

The wood fibers are only slightly compressed with a properly sharpened blade. Whittling with a sharp blade requires much less force, and the knife is also easier to guide. The cut surface in the wood is also clean.

How can you tell if a knife has a blunt edge?

First and foremost, a blunt knife just won't cut well anymore. You often only notice this in direct comparison with a sharp knife. To test whether a knife is blunt, many people run their thumbs across the edge of the blade. This test is not useful because a pointy ridge or a rough cutting edge gives the subjective feeling of a sharp blade. The light test, however, is a visual testing method that allows you to reliably judge the condition of the cutting edge.

If you hold a blunt edge under a strong light source, you will see a light streak on the cutting edge. The light is reflected on the surface of the rounded cutting edge. However, if you hold a sharp blade under the light, no light is reflected. The cutting edge has no surface to reflect the light. That is why no light streak is visible on a sharp cutting edge.

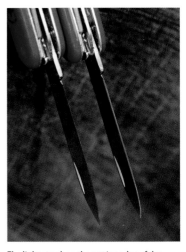

The light streak on the cutting edge of the right-hand knife shows that it's blunt.

The Mini Sharpy

With the Mini Sharpy from Victorinox, even beginners can sharpen their Swiss Army Knife quickly, easily, and safely. Running the blade through the Mini Sharpy just a few times is enough to give the knife a proper sharp edge again. Even blades with a serrated edge can be sharpened with the Mini Sharpy.

The crossed hard metal plates in its interior form a grinding angle of 40°. This fixed grinding angle offers a good compromise between sharpness and durability. Thanks to its handy size and light weight, the inexpensive Mini Sharpy is also ideal for on-the-go use. Ambitious whittlers can apply an additional polish after using the Mini Sharpy to make their blades razor-sharp.

To use the Mini Sharpy, place the knife on its back against a table or other hard surface. Hold the knife by the handle and pull the Mini Sharpy over the blade two to four times with controlled pressure from the handle to the tip of the blade. To even out the blade, run the tool over the edge a few times with less pressure.

Mini Sharpy from Victorinox

40° grinding angle

Pull the Mini Sharpy over the blade with controlled pressure.

A sharp Swiss Army Knife will cut through a piece of paper that is held with two fingers without tearing the paper.

The Right Wood

Green wood is primarily suitable for the projects described in this book: that is, fresh, undried branches and twigs that can be found in the forest or on hedges. Branches that are so dry or rotten that they break easily when bent should be avoided. As a rule of thumb, the fresher the wood, the easier it is to work with.

Not every type of wood is equally suitable for whittling and using with a Swiss Army Knife. Here are some tips, but feel free to experiment with the materials that are available to you where you live. How suitable the wood is for whittling is not the only important criterion. Sometimes the shape, weight, solubility of the bark, size of the pith, and other properties of the wood are more important.

Which Types of Wood Are Best?

The following tips should help you find wood that is common in forests and suitable for whittling with a Swiss Army Knife. It is a definite advantage to know the most common deciduous trees in your area. Most of the projects in this book are made with hazel and elder wood. Soft, light wood is suitable for some projects and heavy, hard wood is recommended for other projects. Beech and oak are hardwoods that are difficult to whittle. Soft types of wood such as poplar or willow are easy to cut, but they fray easily, which, for example, doesn't matter if you're making a boat hull. The following tree species are particularly well suited for whittling: birch, hazel, maple, ash, elder, linden, and alder. Maple and elder wood becomes very hard when dry.

And which types of wood are poisonous? Yew, locust, thuja (cypress family), cherry laurel, and other *Prunus* species, as well as laburnum (golden chain tree), spindle (burning bush), and daphne shrubs are poisonous or have poisonous parts. Health and safety professionals therefore advise against whittling these woods. Due to their bitter tannins, oak and walnut are not suitable for making cooking or eating utensils.

Where to Find the Right Wood

It is strictly forbidden to cut branches from trees in public and private forests and in public parks. However, it shouldn't be a hard to find good whittling materials in nature because there are often many broken branches or fallen trees in the forest that you can use. Often when walking in the forest, you will see leftover sawn-off branches from forest work on the forest floor, or cuttings collected in a pile. Ask the forester or property owner if you are not sure whether you are allowed to use them. Sometimes you will discover a broken tree trunk on walks in the forest. Its splinters and fragments can be used for small boards, a boat hull, for a boomerang, or for other projects. The branches of hazel bushes are great for beginners. They're easy to find and the wood is elastic and not too hard. The bark also easily detaches from the wood so that children can easily remove it or cut beautiful patterns into it.

Acknowledgments

Matthew Worden (*www.matthewworden.com*) is the Roger Federer of photographers—simply the best! Great pictures were and are incredibly important for this book. Thank you for your fantastic commitment, your patience with the moody whittling model, and your enthusiasm for this project. Because we both have children, finding time was not always easy. But when we were on a shoot, we had a great time together. Matthew, this book lives because of your pictures—thank you very much!

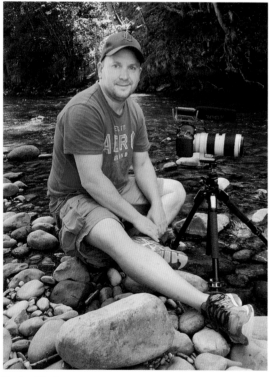

Matthew Worden

My wife and my kids. Finding time to write a book with so many new ideas and projects to develop is hard to plan. It's more spontaneous than a linear process. Spurts of creativity and writing flow don't always occur during work hours. For this reason, it was difficult to coordinate this project with family life. I couldn't hide it when I was thinking about an idea during family time and was physically present but somehow mentally absent. It was not an easy time for me or my family and caused a couple of conflicts. Thank you, dear Silvia, for always supporting me, even in tumultuous times, and for having my back even when you had no energy and were living a less-than-ideal family life. Without you, I would have never been able to do this project the way I did. I hope that our family life will be in calmer waters after this project and that we will emerge stronger as a result. I would also like to thank my children, Janis, Sarah, and Elias. Especially Janis, my older son, who helped me understand whether my projects were kid-friendly or not.

Many thanks to the friends at my employer, **Victorinox**, who were involved in this project as well as the Elsener family from Victorinox. I am proud and thankful to be able to work for Victorinox. Your great trust in me motivates me to do my best every day. I am fully aware that it meant taking a lot of time to work on this book. A very special thanks goes to Gil Sommerhalder. Your support and guidance in many different projects is very valuable to me. The filming days for our YouTube videos are always a highlight and I really enjoy them!

For me, **AT Verlag** is almost like a family. Thank you for your great support. Thank you for your motivating attitude and thank you for your understanding and your ideas when things don't go as planned. I couldn't imagine a better publisher.

Christoph Bürgi, you were my "firefighter" for this project. I was very uncertain when it came to writing and planning the technical implementation of these projects. The fire was blazing and it was the eleventh hour. Thank you very much for your incredible support in the last three weeks. I often got your feedback at times when normal people are asleep—and the fire department is wide awake.

Urs Weber, many thanks to you as well! I benefited greatly from your ideas and solutions. It was very enriching for me to talk to you about the projects. It's great to have you in my life, Urs!

Dear **Mauro Spadin**, I was impressed by your outdoor skills and your creativity. I am glad that I know a place where I can always be sure that there will be really good workshops. Thanks for letting me build upon your idea for the water sprayer.

Regula Immler, I am very grateful that you helped me formulate my thoughts for the foreword and the introduction. I am looking forward to the first whittling course with you and your girls.

Dear **Pascal Zani**, I am very grateful that I can harvest material from the forests in your kingdom throughout the year for my workshops. The tree trunk on the cover is also a St. Margrethler.

Remo Gugolz, keep the "buchhorn" alive (*www. buchhorn.ch*)! Thank you for the inspiration for the two-stick bow, dear Lowland Indians.

Marius Tschirky (*www.jagdkapelle.ch*), I have since received diverse cover versions of your Swiss Army Knife song from different school classes. They give the original a run for its money. Thanks for your inspiration for the balloon saxophone!

Stefan Hinkelmann, (*www.youtube.com/user/ DerMaterialtester*), thank you for your inspiration for the tube slingshot!

Roland Wild, thank you for your inspiration, including a video for the apple slingshot!

Frank Egholm, thank you for letting me use and develop the Indian bow from your book *Das große Buch von Schnitzen* (*The Great Book of Carving*).

Martin and Andy Müller (*www.androma-verlag.ch*), thank you very much, dear Martin, for your great photos and tips on the shingle arrow!

Christoph Trescher, thank you very much, dear Christoph, for your support with the elder wood flute. The afternoon in your workshop in Mogelsberg impressed me very much.

Christoph Kraul (*www.spielzeug-kraul.de*), thank you very much for letting me take the "Trout" project from your father's book and develop it further with a Swiss Army Knife. In my book the project is called "paddle steamer."

Stefan Philippi (*www.werkstatt-am-see.ch*), the reed flute was love at first sight. Thank you, Stefan, for the great project idea!

Sylvia Gianfelice, thank you for your stories and your self-whittled "Dutch Arrow."

Abdy Shamloo (*www.as-art.ch*), thank you for your friendship and the great illustrations for my books.

Taro Gehrmann, thank you for your emotional support. As the author of the book *Feuer machen* (*Making Fire*), you know exactly how great the pressure can be when a book project is nearing completion. It was just so good to talk to you!

Index

Index

About the Author

Felix Immler

Born in 1974 in St. Gallen, Switzerland, trained machine mechanic, social worker, and nature educator Felix is the father of three children. He has been working full-time as a Swiss Army Knife teacher at Victorinox since 2014, where he also offers Swiss Army Knife workshops for children and adults. He runs the YouTube channel "Felix Immler," for which he regularly produces Swiss Army Knife, bushcraft, and survival videos.

🏠 *www.feliximmler.ch*

▶ YouTube *www.youtube.com/feliximmler*

Online Extras

You can find lots of additional whittling material on the website *www.feliximmler.ch*: the comic "Die Schnitz-Kids" about safety rules, worksheets to prepare for the Swiss Army Knife test, diplomas and a Swiss Army Knife song by Marius und die Jagdkapelle (Marius and the Hunting Band). The website also contains videos on the use or production of some Swiss Army Knife projects.